Retreating to Re-Treat

Retreating to Re-Treat

A Performative Encounter at the 'Edge of the Woods'

BY THE COLLECTIVE ENCOUNTER
WITH JILL CARTER

Playwrights Canada Press
TORONTO

First edition: February 2024
Printed and bound in Canada by Imprimerie Gauvin, Gatineau

Jacket design by Jennica Robinson
Copy-edit by Rhonda Kronyk, www.rhondakronyk.ca

Playwrights Canada Press
202-269 Richmond St. W., Toronto, ON M5V 1X1
416.703.0013 | info@playwrightscanada.com | www.playwrightscanada.com

LIBRARY AND ARCHIVES CANADA CATALOGUING IN PUBLICATION
Title: Retreating to re-treat : a performative encounter at the 'edge of the woods' / by The Collective Encounter, with Jill Carter.
Names: Carter, Jill (Jill L.), author. | Collective Encounter, author.
Description: Includes bibliographical references.
Identifiers: Canadiana (print) 20230504280 | Canadiana (ebook) 20230507867 | ISBN 9780369104649 (softcover) | ISBN 9780369104656 (PDF) | ISBN 9780369104663 (EPUB)
Subjects: LCSH: Canadian drama—21st century. | CSH: Canadian drama (English) —21st century
Classification: LCC PS8315.1 R48 2023 | DDC C812/.608—dc23

Playwrights Canada Press staff work across Turtle Island, on Treaty 7, Treaty 13, and Treaty 20 territories, which are the current and ancestral homes of the Anishinaabe Nations (Ojibwe / Chippewa, Odawa, Potawatomi, Algonquin, Saulteaux, Nipissing, and Mississauga / Michi Saagiig), the Blackfoot Confederacy (Kainai, Piikani, and Siksika), néhiyaw, Sioux, Stoney Nakoda, Tsuut'ina, Wendat, and members of the Haudenosaunee Confederacy (Mohawk, Oneida, Onondaga, Cayuga, Seneca, and Tuscarora), as well as Metis and Inuit peoples. It always was and always will be Indigenous land.

We acknowledge the financial support of the Canada Council for the Arts, the Ontario Arts Council (OAC), Ontario Creates, the Government of Ontario, and the Government of Canada for our publishing activities.

Canada Council for the Arts | Conseil des arts du Canada
Ontario Arts Council | Conseil des arts de l'Ontario — an Ontario government agency | un organisme du gouvernement de l'Ontario
Ontario Creates | Ontario Créatif
Canada
Ontario

For Lee Maracle (1950–2021)

Contents

The Wind

SHEILAH MADONNA MORTEL SALVADOR

Is that your laughter or the wind I'm hearing?
A crow maybe,
gently cackling, triumphant,
amused and happy all at once.
I can almost see your halo of silver hair
sparkling from a distance.
And if your voice has a scent,
it would be of smoke and cypress.
Your temper could be treacherous,
but your love was limitless.
You carried with you millenniums
of wisdom, and answers, and more questions.
Of pain and healing that you shared
so honestly and openly with strangers,
settlers, and the sons and daughters of invaders,
and their babies' babies,
because to love also means
to forgive and let go.
You had so many stories and
you were never afraid to be wrong.
You always listened and praised
those who were uncertain and anxious.
But never failed to call out
those who were misguided, and arrogant.
But you were always kind
even when you were intimidating.
A force and a pleasure to reckon with.
Your smile can make one
swoon and bristle with pride,
but that one stare, that raised eyebrow,
could will a sunflower to die.
Your dignity defied the wrinkles of time,

and you wore with grace and honour,
the long years of your curious and fruitful life.
I could listen to you talk all day.
That wicked laugh, your presence
that could be heard from two floors away.
My favourites were your lessons about lust and love.
Whenever I feel hopeless and frustrated,
unloved and rejected, I think of you
sitting at that bar, flashing a smile
at that gentleman with the silver moustache
across the room from you.
You didn't know I was there,
but it was the day you talked about
falling in love at sixty.
Maybe that is why I often mistake
the wind for your laughter.
Why, whenever I see a cedar tree,
I think of you, telling me to let go
and just watch that little tree grow.
To be happy that it's alive and thriving.
Be happy that I am alive and surviving,
refusing to succumb to the pain,
the challenges, just like you did.
And as the wrinkles starts to show
and flourish on my own face,
as what used to be mountains starts to sag
and what use to be silk turns into a desert,
I will think of how you loved,
and how proud you bore the ripples
and rode wildly the earthquakes,
all the while laughing, sometimes
with red lipstick on, hips swaying,
skirt flowing and flirty.
I hear you. I always will.
And for that I will always be grateful.

Acknowledgements

Encounters at the 'Edge of the Woods' and its company of Devisors gratefully acknowledge the invaluable support of all who have so generously supported our endeavors and made both the production and this publication possible. We send out much respect and heartfelt gratitude to John Monahan and Michelle Brownrigg of Hart House, University of Toronto; to Tamara Trojanowska, Antje Budde, Peter Freund, and Paul Stoesser of the Centre for Drama, Theatre and Performance Studies (University of Toronto); to Susan Hill (Chair, Indigenous Studies, University of Toronto); to Stephen Johnson and the Gatherings: Archival and Oral Histories of Performance Project; to Sadie Macdonald, Jamie Chirico, Adrien Hall, Kent Monkman, Jon Johnson, Isabelle Kim, CIUT Radio, and Pamela Klassen (Religious Studies, University of Toronto).

We send out special greetings and heartfelt thanks to Columpa Bobb who supported her mother, our dearly missed collaborator, mentor, and teacher Lee Maracle in guiding us through this process.

And we gratefully acknowledge the Access Programs University Fund provided by the University of Toronto's Division of the Vice-President and Provost and Hart House Theatre; without their support, this project would not have been possible.

To Annie Gibson and Blake Sproule of Playwrights Canada Press, we extend our gratitude for your belief in the Collective Encounter and your enthusiastic support of this project.

Finally, we extend our gratitude to all of those who have paid an incalculable price for us to stand here today. To the ancestors who dreamed of our arrival and to the Elders, Knowledge Keepers, and Kin who ground, nourish and support us, we call, "Chi Miigwetch!"

Miigwetch. Miigwetch. Miigwetch. Miigwetch.

Foreword

JOHN KIM BELL

At the time of these musings in the spring of 2023, Canadians are experiencing an unprecedented number of forest fires not in August, as would be expected, but in May. Inflation continues to plague the country; the climate crisis continues to threaten our existence; there have been 279 mass shootings in the U.S. since January 2023; and a former U.S. president has been arraigned on a variety of criminal charges, yet he is leading in the polls to be re-elected as the president of the country. Another senseless war—this time, in Ukraine—tests our endurance and stretches all of us beyond our safe zones. Humanity seems to be out of control, and democracy appears to be dramatically on the decline.

All of this is a result of decades of unbridled capitalism resulting in massive negative impacts and human suffering. Nowhere has this been underscored better than in the recent theatrical play, *Encounters at the 'Edge of the Woods,'* mounted by Indigenous and non-Indigenous students at the University of Toronto in 2019 under the skilful direction of Dr. Jill Carter, an Indigenous dramaturge and professor at the university.

Encounters, which I attended at its premiere in 2019 at Hart House in Toronto, was a surprise hit with theatregoers for its depth, power, and even entertainment value. Like other attendees, I was bowled over that university students could mount such a professional piece of theatre that moved us, shook us, and underscored the plight of Indigenous Peoples, the plight of humanity, and the plight of our precarious temporal existence on Mother Earth.

Encounters takes us on the journey of Professor Weetahgo, a cannibal figure who derides the spiritual beliefs and doctrinaire of Indigenous Peoples in favour of embracing capitalism and its manifestations of exploitation, colonialism, oppression, and the mistreatment and murder of Indigenous women—the givers of life. The play provides focus of and emphasis on our precarious situation on planet Earth.

Professor Weetahgo wilfully embraces all the evils of capitalism and colonialism visited upon the earth and upon humanity as a way to exist that is preferable to the view held by Indigenous Peoples that everything must be in balance and that nature, not man, is in charge.

Weetahgo, played by Cree actor, writer, and producer Trina Moyan, held the audience spellbound, which was such a delightful surprise as well as powerful and moving. Moyan and the entire cast brought the stark contrast of belief systems into focus and mesmerized the audience with their clarity.

Encounters was well ahead of economist Mark Carney's recent book, *Values: Building a Better World for All*, which attempts to articulate how humanity can and must save itself from climate change. We learn in this profound tome that before the Industrial Revolution, business activity could only be approved by a monarch or government if that activity had some beneficial purpose to humanity. Solely seeking profits was not acceptable until automation and a myriad of technological inventions increased global investment opportunities significantly and spurred unchecked investments that breached any purpose of benefitting society in favour of prioritizing profits as the purpose of commercial activity. Business owners no longer required government approvals—capitalism mutated, and led to the chaos we see today.

Encounters captures how rampant unchecked capitalism that only cares about shareholder earnings has and is devouring the environment, eliminating the middle class, promoting war, and wreaking cultural and physical genocide on Indigenous Peoples. The play situates us as the witness to the phenomenon of murdered and missing Indigenous women, who are the carriers of eco-knowledge and the water protectors. When we kill Indigenous women, we kill the land. We know we are not above of the animals but equal. Against this backdrop, we experience the effects of capitalism where the rich become obscenely richer while the poor become obscenely poorer.

Encounters teaches us that capitalism is not only destroying the planet but all life on it, including humans. Hence, at some point after eating everything else, we will start cannibalizing ourselves. By the end of the play, we experience a clarion and sobering wake-up call, reinforcing and concluding that Indigenous beliefs and our embrace of spiritual matters is relevant and a more correct understanding of our place in nature and on Mother Earth. This is a wake-up call regarding how humanity needs to embrace the protection of nature because protecting nature is really protecting ourselves. It is a message that we all know to be true, but a message that suffers from society's mass denial of our slow, steady, and certain destruction.

Carney embraces this same philosophy by stating that instead of prioritizing shareholder value only, we must return to a way of thinking where all activities have a purpose that is beneficial to humankind. We must focus on the health of the planet; prevent the continuing erosion of the middle class; and reduce the unfair, inequitable manner in which the rich become unnaturally rich while the poor become even poorer and further excluded from society. All the evils of capitalism resulting in mass shootings, war, poverty, and the sickness of Trumpism is not the sudden discovery of Carney, but rather the long-held but ignored beliefs of Indigenous societies from time immemorial. Where we can see some hope is that a prominent mainstream financial figure such as Carney has realized that our Indigenous beliefs have always been valid and are even more important and valid today than anytime before given the threat we collectively face together. If Carney can arrive at this Indigenous conclusion, perhaps others will follow in time.

Encounters at the 'Edge of the Woods' distills, encapsulates, and delivers this powerful message through metaphor in a way that is disturbing, sad, funny—even hilarious—but also deeply meaningful and thought-provoking. *Encounters* should be mounted over and over again and presented across Canada for its timely and superbly wrought thesis. Canadians need to witness this piece as it serves as a cultural bridge between Indigenous beliefs and the mainstream beliefs of settlers. We have arrived at a place and time where Indigenous Peoples and the settlers are not so different and more united in thought than before.

Encounters teaches us that we are not really destroying Mother Earth. Mother Earth will never be destroyed. Instead, we are destroying ourselves. The planet will heal itself as it has over billions of years. The very disappointing, frail, and fragile nature of humanity might end at some point, but the unending spirit of Mother Earth will continue through eternity. Nature will win. We, as an undeserving species, will lose.

We mustn't lose hope, however. Ultimately, Mother Earth will make the correct decisions for us.

A Note About the Artists & the Production

JILL CARTER

With *Encounters at the 'Edge of the Woods,'* a courageous group of scholar-artists has created a survivance-intervention that effects an Indigenous reclamation of territory, placing the settler and Indigenous body, alike, into direct confrontation with a difficult history that has been 'written over' by colonial occupation and invention. They stand with you and me and all the life that is sustained within these territories in a *liminal space*—a space between now and then, a space between now and later. Together, we hover at the edge. In the moment just before creation was activated and the skies blazed with light. In the moment just before the last visible sliver of sun sinks below the horizon. At the beginning of a beginning? At the beginning of an end?

Indigenous protocols, globally, have required us to pause in a liminal space, never touching that place where water kisses land, never venturing into the clearing beyond the dense forest, never stepping off the tarmac until we have sent out the call announcing our presence and intentions and until we have received a response—an invitation to step into the territory of another. Today, we *invite* you to experience and commit yourselves to a process in which these accomplished storytellers have fully invested themselves. We *invite* you to retreat with us into what Métis curator David Garneau has termed "irreconcilable space"—those spaces in which to repair the split mind and from which we might re-encounter each other and the biotas that sustain us with generative action powered by good intention. We *invite* you to refuse the role of occupier and to meet us—not as ones who would push your way onto these territories but as ones who come with good intentions to con-*verse* with us, to shoulder your share of the responsibility, and to fully invest yourselves in the creation of a new treaty-relationship.

This is an incredibly complex task in this historical moment. Canada does not stand, as if for the first time, at the Edge of the Woods. Our Peoples have stood there before: treaties were ratified then violated, promises uttered then broken. The Original Stewards of these territories were subjected to centuries of attempted erasure through extermination or assimilation. Yet, evicted from our homelands and driven into the margins—onto this edge—we continue to assert our existence as Indigenous bodies. And so, for this political act, we continue to be targeted.

Old stories will not be written over. We may cover them with our silence, refusing to lodge their actors in living memory or to breathe life into past misdeeds by speaking them out into the present world; still—like Toronto's fifty buried waterways that, refusing to lie still in their interment, bubble up to gently tease out fissures in city roadways, to breach the foundations of municipal buildings, and to flood the basements of private homes—they continue to plot a course through which new stories unfold and new ghosts are brought into being. Without intentional redress through an ongoing practice of activation—an encounter with the land through which treaty-relationships may be reanimated through remembrance, acknowledgement, and somatic engagement with long-abandoned protocols—our relationships with the soured earth of such places remain troubled, and newly birthed ghosts inherit the bitterness of those who walked this earth before them.

The storytellers you encounter in these chapters and in the play have come to know this and to live their knowledge out in daily practice. I have been humbled by the courage with which they entered this project. I have been heartened by their good intentions. And I continue to be inspirited by their generosity as we travel together.

I celebrate *their* extraordinary work—this *feast*, so lovingly prepared, to nourish and inspirit all of us. And I ask you, "With what intentions do you come to this 'table' at the '*edge of the woods*'"?

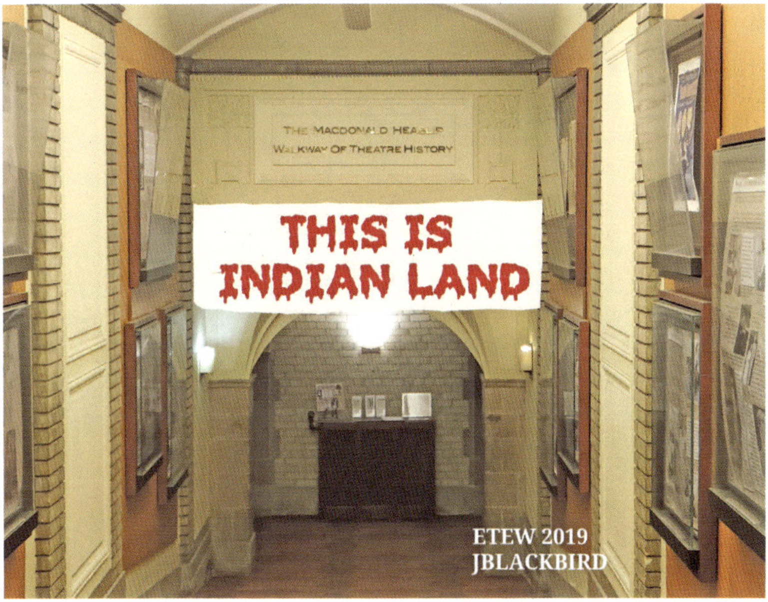

Installation banner by Jenny Blackbird. Photo by Tash Naveau.

"Calling Them In": A Processual 'Encounter'

JILL CARTER AND BRENDA WASTASECOOT
WITH INTERJECTIONS FROM JENNY BLACKBIRD
AND SHARAI MASANGANISE

> *If we are going to move into the time of the eighth fire,*[1] *we have to go together. That means the non-Indigenous people are going to have to keep reaching out to Indigenous people; they must risk asking questions that may expose an uncomfortable ignorance; and we are going to have to practice patience, generosity, and humility, and keep answering questions. And if we do not know the answers, we will have to commit to finding answers together.* (Nolan 129)

INTRODUCTION

JILL: In the fall of 2019, Hart House celebrated its centenary. In 1919, Hart House had been commissioned and gifted to the University of Toronto by the Massey Foundation. Named for Vincent Massey's grandfather Hart, it was established as a place of gathering for students in which they might build social networks while engaging in cultural pursuits outside the lecture halls. Such pursuits have included making and viewing theatrical productions; viewing and discussing original works of art by the Group of Seven, Les Automatistes, and Painters Eleven; spending quiet hours in the Library with a canonical text; studying cartographical masterpieces in the Map Room; and dining in the Great Hall where Milton's Areopagitica (1644) is inscribed on all four walls, reminding U of T community members of a shared responsibility to cherish and defend free speech and free thought.

1 The Anishinaabe once lived on the shores of the Atlantic Ocean. Long before the arrival of the European powers, the prophecy of the Seven Fires was delivered to the Anishinaabe. There was no escaping the colonial encounter that our prophets told us would unfold in seven stages (through seven eras, represented by seven fires). To reduce the impact of first contact (disease and/or outright massacre), the Anishinaabe

On Remembrance Day in Hart House's fiftieth year, the late literary critic Dr. Northrop Frye paid tribute to its purpose and its function with a moving encomium: for him, "Hart House represented the university as a society; it dramatized the kind of life that the university encourages one to live: a life in which imagination and intelligence have a central and continuous function" (Hart House). What remains unaddressed in Dr. Frye's tribute is that entre into this societal crucible in which imagination, artistry, taste, and intelligence were being nourished had been barred to women since its inception.[2] Similarly, it seems "the kind of life" and society that the university's students were being encouraged to carve out for themselves would not include (in any real way) Indigenous Peoples (largely barred from academe by means of the residential school system, Canadian legislation that stripped Status Indians of all Treaty Rights if they did attend an institution of higher learning, and social and economic marginalization—all natural consequences of the racist notions fulminating in the Canadian imaginary).

If, as Thomas King asserts, "The truth about stories is that that's all we are" (2), what becomes of a people and its imagination of self when its storytellers have been muzzled, its publics prohibited, and its history redacted? Since its inception over a century ago, Hart House Theatre has contributed to the development of the storytellers and to the dissemination of the stories that have upheld a heavily edited Canadian imaginary—it *is* Canadian theatre before Canadian theatre could be said to exist, and it has played a significant role in shaping the identity of this nation: William Hutt, Don Harron, Kate Reid, Raymond Massey, Wayne

---

were instructed to migrate west and north away from the sea to sites where food (e.g., wild rice) grows upon the water. As it was prophesied, the agents of colonization have visited greater and greater destruction on the land and peoples with each new era. Today, many Anishinaabe believe that we are now in the time of the seventh fire: in this era, as the prophets foretold, the colonial powers still have an opportunity to consult Indigenous Peoples and to respectfully integrate Indigenous Knowledge Systems into their own practices at every level of existence. If this is done, the prophets promised, both peoples will enter the time of the Eighth Fire together—an era in which all enjoy peace and good life. If the disrespect and disregard for Indigenous Knowledge Systems continue, those ancestors were told, a maelstrom of destruction will ensue, and life on this planet will end.

2 Women were not admitted to Hart House until 1972.

and Schuster, Donald Sutherland, Norman Jewison, and Lorne Michaels all honed their craft upon its boards. Toronto and regional theatres (Crest, Jupiter, Shaw, and Stratford) sprang into existence during the second and third generations of Hart House Theatre's life. Two of Duncan Campbell Scott's[3] plays graced its boards: *Pierre* in 1921 and *Joy, Joy, Joy* in 1926. And Carroll Aikins's three-act play in red-face, *The God of Gods*, was produced by Hart House Theatre in 1922. And yet, in its one hundred years as a cultural crucible for a nation birthed on Indigenous lands, not one Indigenous-authored-or-performed play had ever been seen in Hart House Theatre.

To mark its centenary with a performative declaration through which to signal its participation in the current Canadian project of "Truth and Reconciliation," Hart House Theatre decided to open its one hundredth season with an Indigenous production. In 2018, I was one of several Indigenous academics and culture workers from the University of Toronto community who were consulted about this season-opener. Later that year, representatives of Hart House invited me to facilitate and direct a collectively devised piece that would serve as a performative *intervention* through which its theatre might publicly declare its commitment to the urgent project of re-storying its role as a cultural cornerstone in the colonial edifice that contains us all.

It felt to me, in that historical moment (as it still does), that placing Indigenous bodies on this stage in an attempt to build bridges of understanding by educating a settler audience and/or appealing to settler sympathy was insufficient. Residential school survivors, with Indigenous artists, educators, and activists, have shouldered this work for decades: they have been writing, performing, and speaking out. Yet change continues to be dishearteningly slow. This project, I hoped, might upend colonial complacency and inspire non-Indigenous stakeholders who wish to remediate relations between our peoples to share this work with us. I decided, therefore, to extend an open invitation to non-Indigenous members of

---

3 Duncan Campbell Scott (Poet Laureate of Canada) served as both a Treaty Commissioner (Treaties 6 and 9) and as the Superintendent of Indian Affairs in the early twentieth century. He viewed "Indian Policy" in Canada as a mechanism with which to legislatively eradicate all Status Indians in Canada. In 1923, he amended the Indian Act to make it compulsory for all Status children seven to fifteen years of age to attend residential schools in Canada.

the campus community to enter into this project and, hence, into an honest encounter with the lands upon which our campus rests—with its difficult history of harmful research practices, damaging pedagogies, and exclusionary policies—and, most importantly, with the survivors of ongoing colonial violence who navigate the University of Toronto and whose lives, apart from the institution, continue to be affected by its outputs and the legislative policies these underpin.

Entering this project, I was wrestling with a tangle of questions: What dramaturgical methods might I employ to safely navigate the frontier between witness and voyeur? How might I ensure that the Indigenous bodies on the stage were not performing as fodder for colonial consumption? How might I ensure that the burdensome work of relationship-building was shared equitably between Indigenous and non-Indigenous company members and, ultimately, between storytellers and witnesses alike? To what extent would the specifically Indigenous methodologies and dramaturgical structures with which I had chosen to work serve the project of relationship-building in that historical moment?

Although, at the time, I did not consciously associate this project with the terms "Eighth Fire production"[4] and/or "Eighth Fire initiative," both speak to the spirit and intent of *Encounters*, which sought to engage Indigenous and non-Indigenous storytellers in a project through which to collaboratively explore and intervene upon the national story that has shaped us and our attitudes toward each other. This project would, I believed, afford an opportunity for a generative "partnership" within which to process fraught histories and difficult knowledge and through which, perhaps, to enter a space of "solidarity" (see Nolan 118).

---

4 I first encountered this term in Algonquin playwright-director Yvette Nolan's 2015 publication of *Medicine Shows: Indigenous Performance Culture*. Here, Nolan identifies *The Book of Jessica* (1997), a celebrated play birthed from a fraught collaboration between Linda Griffiths and Maria Campbell, as an early example of an "Eighth Fire production." Nolan imagines the eighth fire as a generative space of artistic collaboration between Indigenous and non-Indigenous culture workers—a space within which alliances between Indigenous Peoples and Canadians may be birthed, nurtured, and strengthened, and from which collaborative acts of "solidarity" may be performed (Nolan 118).

BRENDA: I entered the Collective Encounter as a storyteller and educator. I had been in an acting group before, and I had found it to be very empowering, so I was interested to see where this would take me. As the project began, I was apprehensive, as I usually am when working with non-Indigenous people. I like the term "cautiously optimistic." That's me. I've learned to expect little. And was I surprised at how much they [fellow cast members] brought out?! At times I was impatient with them, but gradually I saw myself as their grandmother, too. In the times of our ancestors, they parented all the children, not just their biological children or grandchildren. They fed all the hungry children in their homes and communities, hunting camps, and winter trapline lodges. It mattered very little what color they were; this was the level of kindness and generosity of our people. Working on this project was a very healing process for me. I felt like my story was being taken seriously, and everyone was responding or adding to it.

JILL: This introduction recounts the journey of a group of scholar-artists who set themselves the task of crafting a survivance-intervention[5] that would affect an Indigenous reclamation of territory, placing settler and Indigenous bodies alike into direct confrontation with a difficult history that has been overwritten by colonial occupation and invention. We attempted to imagine and then carve out a space in which to encounter each other—a space in which to consider the project of relational repair between Indigenous and non-Indigenous Peoples within a context of broken trust; ongoing dismissal of Indigenous Knowledge Systems; and continuing assaults on Indigenous individuals, families, and communities.

The conversation that follows finds utterance in the wake of many valiant (albeit infelicitous) attempts to forge efficacious Eighth Fire productions—attempts that predate *Encounters at the 'Edge of the Woods'* by as many as four decades (see Nolan 118–122). Throughout the conversations and reflections in this book, we attempt to articulate the beginnings of a process through which the Collective Encounter cobbled together its own

5 The Anishinaabe author-scholar Gerald Vizenor crafted the term "survivance" as a crucible in which "survival" and "resistance" are fused into one ideological phenomenon. It entails, in Vizenor's words, "an active sense of presence, the continuance of native stories, not a mere reaction, or a survivable name [. . .] Survivance stories [then] are renunciations of dominance, tragedy and victimry" (vii).

Eighth Fire creation. In this, we hope to contribute to existing scholarship around such collaborations and to offer our own address to settler-scholar Melissa Poll's call for "studies that articulate and compare protocols within Indigenous-settler rehearsal processes" on Turtle Island (394).

CALLING THEM IN

> *Canada is a test case for a grand notion—the notion that dissimilar peoples can share lands, resources, power, and dreams while respecting and sustaining their differences. The story of Canada is the story of many such peoples, trying and failing and trying again, to live together in peace and harmony.* (*Report of the Royal Commission on Aboriginal People*, qtd. in Nolan 355)

JILL: South of the forty-ninth parallel, a war began in 1754 between the French and the British for control of this continent. It concluded with the Treaty of Paris in 1763, at which France surrendered the Ohio Valley in the east and the Mississippi in the west to the British. Following the ratification of the Treaty of Paris, King George III produced a Royal Proclamation that declared British title to the lands between the Mississippi and the Atlantic Ocean and from Nova Scotia to Georgia. George III also stipulated that, although the British now held title to much of the continent, European settlement would only be permitted on lands east of the Appalachians. Lands to the west of this mountain range were to be reserved for uncontested occupation by Indigenous Peoples. Of course, as more and more European settlers poured in, the 1763 boundary line was gradually moved westward to make room for British occupation and settlement.

In 2015, the Truth and Reconciliation Commission of Canada released its final report outlining the history and enumerating the ill effects of the residential school system in the lands now referred to as "Canada." Appended to this report are ninety-four *calls* to Canada, its institutions, and its citizens to perform a series of actionable tasks—the purpose of which is to operationalize the remediation of the fraught relationship that exists between Indigenous Peoples and this nation-state. Included in these is a call (45) to Canada to craft a new Royal Proclamation—a Royal Proclamation of Reconciliation—which will retain King George

III's original recognition of Indigenous rights to sovereign nationhood and territories upon which to govern their nations. As my colleague and co-writer Dr. Brenda Wastasecoot has noted, the Calls to Action constitute a "calling in" of all Canadians to actively participate in the delicate task of relational repair.

BRENDA: I like the idea of "calling them in"; it is like a ceremony. We call in our ancestors when we start our feasting and dancing, for example. We call in those who are here to participate, to bring their thoughts and stories to the project.

JILL: It was Call 45 that I wished to address with this project—a project I envisioned as a collectively devised address of this imagined future. Such an address, I anticipated, would carry its participants into spaces in which they were compelled to see, remember, and respond to a tangled history of settlement, to long-suppressed histories, to buried waterways, to silenced voices, and to ravished earth. This was a project that would require willing bodies, open hearts, and absolute commitment to the task at hand. This was a project that would demand full investment and active participation by non-Indigenous individuals who have benefited from living, learning, and working on stolen lands. This was, at the end of the day, a community-building enterprise and not an opportunity for career-building.

I am an urban woman through whom Anishinaabe and Ashkenazi bloodlines flow. My praxis and passions lie in exploring the operationalization of Nation-specific Indigenous Knowledge Systems, linguistic structures, and aesthetic principles within the crafting of contemporary Indigenous performative events. The works that I make, in which I am involved, or that I have been privileged to explore fly in the face of accepted conventions of theatre-making as taught in North American conservatories or as practiced on the public stage. Hence, I chose to dispense with auditions; instead, I sent out a call throughout the University of Toronto community and various Indigenous organizations within the GTA offering a brief overview of the proposed project and inviting all interested individuals regardless of experience or formal training to attend an information session at which pizza would be consumed and discussion would ensue. I began by speaking to the spirit and intent of the project and describing the process that would guide us. Then, after offering a rough rehearsal schedule, outlining what little compensation I could offer, and identifying the ways in which people could participate (as either devisers, deviser-performers, production personnel, stage management, or installation artists), I then asked those present to share what interested them about this project. Finally, I invited those who could commit to the project and wished to be involved to provide their names, contact information, and any dates during which they would be unavailable, and I invited these individuals to list the area(s) in which they would like to be involved (again, regardless of experience or formal training).

Ultimately, all individuals who attended and committed themselves to the project were assigned to the role(s) they had chosen. Some signed up for two positions. For instance, lead sound designer Uri Livne-Bar also served the project as a deviser-performer; deviser-performer Sarah Michaels volunteered to record and transcribe the improvisatory sessions of her non-Indigenous colleagues; Cree artist-scholar Brenda Wastasecoot created two projections and the Cree Woman's Song for the show, while nehiyaw artist and language keeper Jenny Blackbird created a series of multimedia works for the pre-show installation. Both of these fiery artists were also deviser-performers for *Encounters*.

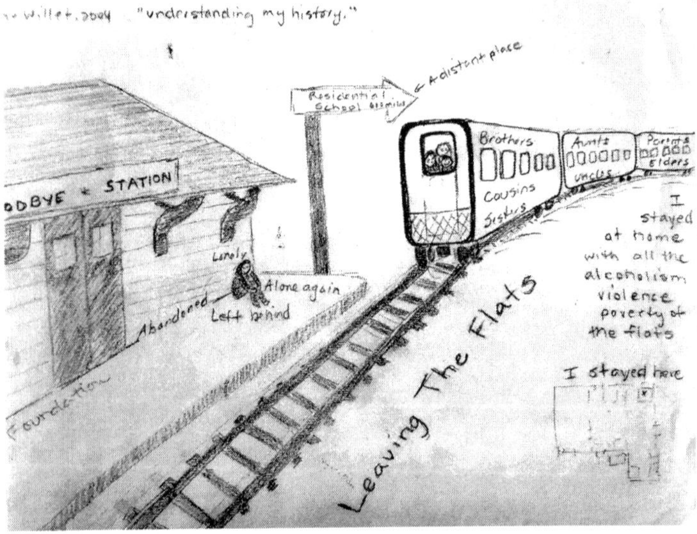

Projected image of "The Goodbye Station" created for *Encounters* by Brenda and Dayle Wastasecoot. Photo by Brenda Wastasecoot.

BRENDA: The Goodbye Station is a drawing my daughter Dayle Wastasecoot and I did together, as I was trying to capture what it was like to see my siblings leaving on the train every September to return to residential school. It was always a lonely time for me and for my parents; we would not see them again until July or an occasional Christmas visit (if they were allowed to come home). I did feel abandoned by them because I didn't understand the workings of this government policy. So, I didn't understand their predicament of having to leave their baby sister behind. The drawing shows the deeply embedded railway, which was put there by Canada to create easier access to our lands, and resources, and children. The words *brothers, sisters, cousins, aunts, uncles* on the image of the train tell of the many generations of children being taken and of so many who would never return.

The Cree Woman's Song, from Manitoba, came from a gathering of women at a cultural teachings camp with Elder Stella Blackbird. I was hired to spend this weekend with the women to be a listener. We sat around the fire at night and sang with our drums. Before that, I had been working on a song with Dr. Fyre Jean Graveline and MaryAnn Whitefish in their healing lodge near Brandon, Manitoba. We were singing, in Cree, a song of strength for the students in the First Nations and Aboriginal Counseling (FNAC) program at Brandon University. This is where the inspiration for this Cree Woman's Song came from.

iskwewuk! waniskak! nipawik! boomithdek! nikimook!

Every time I sing it, I can hardly hold back the tears, as it is a wake-up song, and a calling in of our strength as a people. This song calls upon us to take charge of our lives, and to gather up all our ancestral strength so that we can join our voices together to end violence against Indigenous women and girls.

I sang this song at my niece Angeline's funeral. She had taken her life in August of 2020. We have lost many women and girls due to violence; we have lost many of our young people due to suicide. We need to work together, find our voices in all ways of healing and community-building work. Acting in theatre, especially Indigenous theatre, has always been healing for me; we need more of this in schools and universities across Canada.

TOGETHER APART ON STORIED LAND

> *Indigenous protocols globally have required us to pause in a liminal space never touching that place where water kisses land, never venturing into the clearing beyond the dense forest, never stepping off the tarmac until we have sent out the call announcing our presence and intentions and until we have received a response—an invitation to step into the territory of another. Today, [we] invite you to refuse the role of occupier, to meet us not as ones who would push your way onto these territories, who would extract Indigenous Knowledge for your own purposes but as ones who come with good intentions to con-*verse *with us, to shoulder your share of the responsibility, and to fully invest yourselves in the creation of a new treaty-relationship.* (Carter 195)

JILL: During the planning stages of this project, I envisioned us in constant communion—doing this work together: as we would be weaving our stories in the tradition of Spiderwoman Theater,[6] we would begin (as they do) with all collaborators in the room from the first day, "Coming in with ideas and then really talking and talking and talking" (Miguel, qtd. in Yazzie). But during that year, as I prepared for rehearsals, I began to wonder if this was not a naïve impulse for such a project as this. We were *not* a pre-existing collective with established relationships. We were not coming into this work with a shared worldview and shared

6 Founded by Guna Rappahannock theatre-maker Muriel Miguel with her sisters Gloria Miguel and Lisa Mayo, Spiderwoman Theater is both the longest-running Indigenous theatre company and the longest-running feminist theatre troupe in North America. Devised by Muriel Miguel, Spiderwoman Theater's Storyweaving Practice is a distinct methodology that governs the dramaturgical structure and performed transmission of this company's play texts on the contemporary stage. However, it is important to acknowledge that the practice of Storyweaving predates written history. It has been (and remains) specific to tribal storytellers across this continent. The reclamation, then, of this aesthetic legacy by contemporary Native storytellers is a crucial act of recovery, which imagines and architects a functional framework for a poetics of re-worlding, which is being adopted and adapted by artists from myriad Nations to create works (on the page and stage) that affect the healing, transformation, and survivance of their communities.

experiences—even of historical moments that we had all lived through. We all hoped that the relationships that came out of this process would be grounded in true respect and reciprocity, and I, for one, hoped that these relationships would be *lasting*. I hoped too that each of us would come away from this experience *transformed*. And for these goals to be achieved, absolute honesty was required. Trust would have to be built. Indigenous and non-Indigenous participants alike needed to be able to confront difficult knowledge, to engage in hard conversations, to wrestle together with our fears, our hopes, and our most cherished biases and assumptions. In the words of Filipina company member Sheilah Madonna Salvador during an initial company discussion, "It's hard to find a safe space, but you can create a brave space" (see Arao and Clemens 135). Certainly, bravery would be required of us if we were to break the dam together. But in forcing a premature togetherness, I could either be courting dysfunction and micro-aggression, or a politely false, *distinctly Canadian* encounter in which any possibility of authentic relations would be lost.

Before relationship could be re-storied, we needed to retreat from each other into what Métis curator David Garneau has termed "irreconcilable spaces of Aboriginality"—spaces in which to severally identify our role in and undertake the work of relational repair (see Garneau 21–41). And so, I began to curate these spaces of preparation, discussion, and devising, working alternately with Indigenous-identifying participants and then with non-Indigenous participants, finally bringing both groups together to share their reflections, their objectives, the work they had done, and their insights. For me, these spaces of restricted gathering were (and continue to be) irreconcilable only in their non-negotiability. Indigenous storytellers require—if not a safe space—a saf*er* space in which to wholeheartedly plunge into their work. Non-Indigenous storytellers require the same: they needed to reveal themselves, to make mistakes, perhaps, without wounding others, to correct such errors and see with new eyes. During this period, I thought of these spaces as "spaces of condolence." My colleague Dr. Signy Lynch has referred to such spaces as "spaces of affinity."[7] Howsoever one might term them, such spaces offer

---

7 I am most grateful to Dr. Signy Lynch, who has introduced me to the work and ideas of 1960's artist activist Ben Morea who was the co-founder of Up Against the

a containment unit in which to wrestle with difficult knowledge, to work through it, and to consider what may be required enacted to remediate its consequences.

BRENDA: The irreconcilable spaces are important because it gives us Indigenous actors a chance to share how we're really feeling, and what we are really thinking as we work with non-Indigenous actors, without having to worry about how this might offend someone. This would be good to introduce as a process of working together in the early meetings or the auditions.

JILL: Brenda Wastasecoot brought this aspect of "condolence" into the spaces in which the irreconcilable had been collapsed and both groups gathered to share the work that we had done. It was she who reminded me of the importance of sharing our lives and struggles with each other and ensuring that each company member knew that life's baggage did not have to be "left outside the door." All members could bring their whole selves into the room and trust that their colleagues would listen with compassion and respect and would offer unconditional support. As our work intensified and the days passed, I often entered our room anxiously focused on the task at hand. Brenda slowed the pace, instituting company "sharing times." These sharing times, which preceded or concluded rehearsals, were not imposed as a regular part of our sessions together, as we wanted to ensure that company members would not feel obligated to speak. Instead, the model that Brenda introduced was organic, and these sharing times were instigated by company members when and as they had need.

BRENDA: In that same spirit of supporting one another, it's also important to have the sharing times, or debriefing circles. I remember the group really liking that process as well. I can imagine that just being heard while we are taking some of the oppressor roles or victimized personas would bring up some feelings for each of us. It felt good to be able to say, "I have been dealing with this or that" or "Here's how

---

Wall, Motherfucker! An "affinity group" of "decentralized activists" committed to societal change (see Fahs 38).

it's going for me while I'm acting as a mean white man." For myself, as an Indigenous woman, I felt more supported in being given time and attention from the group. At the time, I was trying to balance a few things: family, work, and the play. So, it was a good way to start our sessions and, also, a good way to end them.

JILL: From its very beginnings, the devising process rooted itself in Call and Response crafted in irreconcilable space. We began by placing our bodies into encounter, first with the waters atop which the University of Toronto's downtown campus so placidly rests and then with the rich earth and hard clay into which the campus infrastructure and decorative landscaping has rooted itself. From these early encounters and throughout the discussion/devising process, we dissolved the artificial barriers between performers, designers, and production personnel. Everybody on the team had come to tell a story—with body, with voice, with light, with projections, with the configuration of the stage, with sound. And so, all were invited into the land-based work, and all participated in the story-creation sessions that followed. Ultimately, stories and fragments of story, generated by designers and stage managers, were integrated into the final script. And this, I believe, deepened their ownership and personal investment in this project of relational repair.

nehiyaw artist Jenny Blackbird, for instance, had joined the project as an installation artist. As she notes below, she had no desire to perform. However, as she became increasingly enmeshed in the project, and as her ideas materialized to weave themselves into the greater whole, it became apparent to all that her voice, breath, and embodied presence were required to animate her creations, transforming her creations into scene partners, rather than set dressing.

JENNY BLACKBIRD: The Candy Girl stand was fun to make. Originally, I didn't plan on being in the production or on stage; I just wanted to contribute some visual art to the project. I thought about the food that Indigenous Peoples would eat pre-contact: from the land, foraged, hunted, planted/harvested, or fished from various waters. The food post-contact and especially in the twentieth and twenty-first centuries is not as good as what our ancestors ate back before assimilation really took hold. I thought it would be fun. Instead of being a cigarette girl with a cigarette tray, I could be the Candy Girl. I was envisioning having candy in my little cigarette-girl tray—or even fake treaties. During our workshopping discussions, we had a whole discussion about having fake treaties to hand out to every audience member to sign.

Jenny Blackbird as Candy Girl (pre-show installation). Photo by Jill Carter.

I proposed setting up a "Candy Girl" stand in the lobby. On one side I hand painted the five "white gifts": flour, sugar, salt, milk, and lard—all the ration foods the government gave our ancestors. These foods aren't so great for anybody, but they really affect Indigenous Peoples' health in awful ways. On the other side I painted wild game meat, fish, berries, corn, beans, squash, and wild rice. All the good, nutritious foods that our ancestors ate. Those are the foods that we still do eat, and they are so much better for our health, and I know that it is getting increasingly hard to get fresh fish, game meat, or find safe spots to forage, plant, and harvest. I even made a pamphlet that was very tongue-in-cheek because Candy Girl is very clownish, and she was asking you whether you would prefer to eat the five white gifts which may cause you harm, or would you rather eat the good foods from the land and from the waters that are not genetically modified.

JILL: What stories do these lands hold? What have they seen? How might we develop a somatic apprehension of the ways in which we have storied and been storied by the buried histories communicated to us in whispers, in unbidden impulse, in sudden, seemingly irrational rushes of emotion? How might our very bones echo with the land's utterances? How might we train our blood to sing, our breath to quicken, and our nerve endings to jump to attention in response to the call of the earth? The act of beginning the rehearsal process by initiating a reclamation of intimacy with the lands of which Indigenous Peoples have been dispossessed—from which we have been severed and barred—is an act that refuses Western dramaturgical models and colonial epistemological convention. The urgency of reinstituting projects that privilege land-based teaching, learning, and creating cannot be overstated in this time of ongoing genocide and escalating ecocide.

On the manicured grounds of our downtown campus, we listened for the whisper of befouled and buried waters, we enumerated the details and recounted the spirit and intent of the 1876 Indian Act on the grounds of Sir John A. Macdonald's home from 1876 to 1879.[8] We remembered nutritional

8 This house (the Macdonald-Mowat House) is located on St. George Street, just north of College Street. It is now the home of the School of Graduate Studies at the University of Toronto.

experiments dreamed to life in campus laboratories and activated in residential schools. And we retold stories of murderous research adventures—buried stories on whose bones the intellectual life of a nation rests. Lingering, some spoke in hushed voices, some sang to the land, some listened.

BRENDA: For me, it is urgent to get our stories out there, so that Canadian audiences can understand the critical things that are still happening to us. The genocide is ongoing—we are in urgent need of housing, healthcare, mental health services, food, safe spaces just to be who we are, and the list goes on.

JILL: In our land-based sessions, the Indigenous artists took more time with the process than did the non-Indigenous artists. Where it felt as if the non-Indigenous artists were deftly processing facts from a human voice (mine) to feed the intellect, absorbing aesthetic impressions from our surroundings to feed inspiration, and then eagerly pushing forward to gather more, the Indigenous artists *lingered*. They were visiting relatives and listening intently to the other-than-human voices greeting them from stone walls, manicured green spaces, and paved-over lots. Whether they were Indigenous to Turtle Island or to other colonized lands, these artists seemed to listen with greater urgency than did their non-Indigenous counterparts. And their response was more immediate, as *they spoke offerings* through their entire organisms—offerings that emerged from lived experience and from the knowledge of their responsibility to ancestors, compatriots, and those to come. Offerings upon which they would continue to build and which they would continue to adorn with all the gifts belonging to their craft.

BRENDA: When given a voice or a platform to be heard, I have always spoken out to anyone who would listen, it was something I always felt was my responsibility, as there were so many more children who would never be able to speak; so many children died from my community, by violence, alcohol poisoning, house fires, or suicide.

JILL: By contrast, the response from the non-Indigenous artists (also invited to spend as much time as they wished on each site we visited) was far less immediate. Perhaps the reticence these young artists initially displayed was engendered by a desire to listen without speaking?

A thoughtful impulse—and often the correct impulse in many situations. Here, however, truthful, organic response was requisite. We were, after all, working through and reconciling ourselves to *irreconcilable truths* in a space of affinity—a safer space in which difficult knowledge, once acknowledged, might be met with condolence.

During our land-based work, I learned a crucial lesson about the intentional use of irreconcilable space or spaces of condolence within the Eighth Fire production. As Jennifer Alicia Murrin and Grace Phan write later in this book, such spaces can be regarded as a 'punishment' to non-Indigenous individuals—signaling a lack of trust. Indeed, I have sometimes encountered non-Indigenous individuals who attempt to breach Indigenous space, and I have had to turn them away with the reminder that once we have all accomplished the work we need to do within these spaces, we will all be together again. Interestingly, the reverse is not true. Neither the Indigenous members of this collective nor Indigenous students I have engaged in this work have ever expressed or acted on a desire to insert themselves into spaces designated for the work to be accomplished by their non-Indigenous colleagues.

Issues around métissage and intersectionality also complicate matters. Murrin and Phan, for example, point to moments in which two spaces were not sufficient: in such moments Murrin, who is both L'nu and European, was not always sure which space to choose. Finally, within the non-Indigenous or settler group of company members, there were, of course, newcomers to these territories who had had to leave the lands to which they are Indigenous to escape the depredations of the colonial project. These individuals brought with them experiences of mission schools (rather than residential schools), of violence, racism, and myriad assaults to their dignity.

SHARAI MASANGANISE: I attended a primary boarding school in Zambia, where my parents had gone from Zimbabwe to train as teachers at a mission teacher training college. The college was run by The Dutch Reformed Church with its headquarters then in South Africa. Professor Carter asked me to narrate my experience of boarding school at such a tender age. As I told my story, my vision immediately went to the dormitories and the diet at the school. The toilets, as we called them, were outside of the dormitory and it was a walking distance before you reached them. If you woke up in the night and wanted to go to the toilet you would ask if anyone else wanted to go. If no one replied, then you would walk by yourself in the dark as the lights were turned off at a certain time. I remember the smelly toilets with feces all over the place; I remember that you had to make sure you did not step on the filth.

Sharai Masanganise during tech-dress rehearsal at Hart House Theatre, September 2019. Photo by Scott Gorman for Hart House Theatre.

During our regular meetings and sharing our stories I found out that the Indigenous members who had siblings or relatives who attended residential school shared similar experiences with me. Even those who did not attend residential or boarding school, their experience connected us to colonialism, systematic segregation. I started thinking about what education was all about. I still question the relevance of education and what about the knowledge itself acquired as I venture in my graduate studies into something called *education*.

BRENDA: Later in the play (Scene 9), I tell the story of my siblings catching the train and leaving me at the Churchill Hotel door, where my parents were drinking at the time. This is a sliver of a larger story about the impacts of the residential school system. But this is the memory that surfaced for me when working with Jill. She drew this out of me by directing me to go to that place and reveal that which I have never revealed before. I was a little worried how it would look to the audience. I didn't want to make my family look bad. But it was the memory that I was confronted with and really needed to bring out. With this "siblings leaving story" I tried to show the audience the impossible situations we found ourselves in as children.

Left to right: Pesch Nepoose, Brenda Wastasecoot, and Melanie Laking during tech-dress rehearsal at Hart House Theatre, September 2019. Photo by Scott Gorman for Hart House Theatre.

JILL: Through the responses, offerings, and reflections of such artists, it dawned on me that my crudely carved spaces (Indigenous and non-Indigenous to Turtle Island) were insufficient. As I also teach Indigenous Studies courses, which are replete with difficult knowledge, to mixed groups in my courses at the University of Toronto, I have since begun to curate multiple spaces allowing students (whose experiences are intersectional) to determine which spaces to enter on which given occasion. Such spaces include those devoted to individuals who identify as (a) Indigenous to Turtle Island, (b) racialized, (c) otherwise marginalized, and (d) non-racialized and able-bodied. These spaces of condolence have worked to good effect, and I continue to reflect upon the work accomplished within these spaces and to refine their curation in accordance with the work to be accomplished and with the individuals involved.

The site at which I first realized that two spaces might not be enough was at a large tree that is regally poised above the buried waters of Taddle Creek at the eastern corner of Hart House's south-facing entrance. Here, during the non-Indigenous land-based work, company member Katia Café-Fébrissy forced a halt to the onward momentum of the group. Katia is of French-Caribbean heritage and emigrated to Canada from Paris, France, where she was born. Growing up amidst the descendants of those who colonized her own ancestors and expropriated their lands and bodies, Katia carries the dis-ease of the colonized—of epigenetic trauma[9]—in her flesh, blood, and bone. Katia approached this tree, circling carefully, gently touching its aged trunk, and engaged in an act of deep listening and unselfconscious response as, with tears streaming down her face, she began to speak in disjointed verse. And it was as if the tree had chosen her and was speaking through her, bearing witness to unspeakable crimes against humanity that have so often been conceived within and underwritten by the institutions of higher learning within which the intellectual life of the colonizing power lives: "The beauty of the tree is only there to cover our wrongdoings. Bodies are upside down. Cores stitched back together [. . .] I hear cries; I hear screams; I smell their last breath."[10]

9 Readers who wish to understand more about the epigenetic trauma carried through generations of Indigenous, racialized, and white bodies within the confining colonial framework that has contained us and our forebears for centuries are encouraged to consult the works of African American trauma-therapist Resmaa Menakem. I first met Menakem through a podcast—a lovely and lively place to begin: "Notice the Rage; Notice the Silence," *On Being with Krista Tippet*, 4 June 2020, https://onbeing.org/programs/resmaa-menakem-notice-the-rage-notice-the-silence/.

10 Later in the rehearsal process, Katia Café-Fébrissy and I returned to this tree with Sarah Michaels (who had also been deeply affected, compelled to linger, and to offer support to Katia). Katia opened herself to further encounter with this natural body, and the fuller piece that eventually emerged from this work was woven into the final production.

"TALK AND TALK AND TALK" IN IRRECONCILABLE SPACE

JILL: Insufficient as two spaces may have been, they were not entirely without benefit. Indeed, it was within these spaces of sharing, processing, and early story-creation with Lee Maracle and her daughter Columpa Bobb that we located the seed from which this project would grow. During our first discussion in irreconcilable space, Brenda Wastasecoot remarked upon the composition of photographs and paintings rendered by settler-artists. "We are always on the margins," she observed. "We are always at the edge." We knew that we wanted to reflect upon our own experiences within the pedagogical institution, and even here, we could see that the spatial composition of those settler-rendered photographs and paintings told an enduring story: at the University of Toronto, the Office of Indigenous Student Services (First Nations House), the Indigenous Studies Program, and the Centre for Indigenous Studies are all housed in a repurposed dairy on the western boundary of the campus. In life, as in art, we were—even while entering the second decade of the twenty-first century to welcome in an era of reconciliation—still hovering at the margins.

Our mandate became very clear: the Indigenous storytellers sought not only to "flip the script" but also to flip the space, to flip perception and, finally, to craft protocols to meet each other at the "edge." Hence, we devised a welcoming ceremony, thereby flipping conventional notions of spatial occupancy and conventional notions of spaces from which to gaze. Indigenous company members gathered on a studio-stage (where they had never been invited to perform), not to be witnessed but instead to witness. Their non-Indigenous colleagues introduced themselves and their families from the house; then, shared the spirit and intent with which they were coming into this project before being welcomed by their Indigenous colleagues to step over the edge and to join them in the space of storytelling as collaborators in this project. This event did not affect an immediate dissolution of "irreconcilable space"; nor was it meant to. It, rather, highlighted the necessity of carving an edge from which to call out and to respond, from which to ask consent and to grant it, and from which to alternatively meet to re-treat with or to retreat from each other with a promise to meet again and again and again.[11]

Through such exercises, we began to understand that in leaving irreconcilable spaces to gather as an entire team, we were carving out a third space in which to meet again at the edge of the woods and begin a process of re-treating together in this historical moment. The trick would be to replicate this space in production to bring witnesses into this liminal space—a space between now and then, a space between now and later. At

---

11 When this rite of welcoming ceremony was concluded, the entire company embarked upon its first discussion outside of irreconcilable space. Here, we were to share our queries, reflections, and insights and to begin to share some of the stories we wished to explore. Here, again, the spatial script and the ways in which we inscribed ourselves upon that "script" in relation to others in the room offered a new lesson that speaks to patience—to readiness. After a break for refreshments and private reflection, I gathered the group and refrained from any instructions pertaining to how they might position themselves within the space. Some grabbed chairs: some sat on the floor; some stood alone; some clustered in small groups of two or three. They took the space as they wished, and the discussion began. We had been speaking openly and eagerly for almost thirty minutes when a non-Indigenous cast member suggested that we all position ourselves within a circle. I had my doubts. Recent experiences in previous mixed groups had caused me to ask several questions: What is a circle? When is a circle not a circle? Was this too much too soon? Nonetheless, I did not object, and all company members readjusted their positions so that all were now sitting in a large circle. But once we were there, it seemed that speech stalled. The ease and openness that had characterized this gathering only moments before had been replaced by a stiffness in some, a palpable wariness in others. As the facilitator and notetaker, I now found that I had to expend a great deal of energy in encouraging dialogue—in "breaking the dam," as it were. Afterwards, several company members (Indigenous and non-Indigenous) spoke to me privately about the discomfort and even a growing resentment they had felt as they sat in this inorganic configuration that was supposed to signify a unity and trust that was only beginning to blossom. I have since reflected on Poundmaker Cree Playwright-Director Floyd Favel's concept of the "artificial tree" (see Favel 69–73). It is too easy to dress up a set—to offer a representation of a ceremonial moment; for some time, it has been too easy to purchase or fabricate "authentic" ceremonial objects or regalia to suggest the promise of a spiritually profound experience. But, as Favel cautions, such representations (well-meaning as they may be) offer nothing to participant or witness because they "[have] no roots, and no animating spirit" (71). One might as well smudge over a dead fire. This again is a micro-lesson in relational repair—a reminder to walk softly and with good intent. When the time is right, the circle will form itself.

the beginning of a beginning? At the beginning of an end? The questions for which we had gathered to seek answers concerned themselves with the urgent project of relational repair in the present moment through redress of past and ongoing violations and genocidal acts. We sought to imagine into being a world in which future generations of Indigenous Peoples and Canadians might begin a process of conciliation powered by acknowledgement, redress, and reciprocity.

SIDEBAR: FLIPPING THE SCRIPT—SPATIAL REPAIR

JILL: Quite early in the process, I learned a crucial and empowering lesson at the edge of the *institutional* woods. Our company had been assured by Hart House and Hart House Theatre that smudging would be permitted to its members at any time, in any place throughout rehearsals. During the first week of rehearsal in July 2019, we discovered this was not the case. Intentions were good. A promise had been made. But, it seemed, the promise came with conditions. In some rooms, we could smudge; in others, we could not. In some rooms, we could smudge in certain areas and after certain preparations had been made; in other rooms, no provisions had to be met. As we did not have a designated rehearsal space throughout the process, we had to ensure that we understood the guidelines for each space we occupied. We were grateful for the support and the spaces provided, so we were gracious and compliant. But on one emotionally fraught evening, in a space where smudging was not permitted, patience strained to breaking.

Now, on an evening of broken promises and frustrated spiritual need, in a space where smudging was forbidden, Stó:lō Cree-Métis author, educator, and activist Lee Maracle deftly overwrote another well-worn script and offered us a potent teaching. Instead of seeking permission to conduct ceremony in a colonial edifice, she suggested that we regard this site as not yet appropriate for such undertakings. She told us that this site needed to be readied before it could be deemed a fitting space in which to burn the medicines. In this spirit, Maracle carved out an *irreconcilable edge* at the building's outer threshold; from there, she oversaw the smudging ceremony with Anishinaabe scholar and Knowledge Keeper Verne Ross. Suddenly, institutional permission to exercise a cultural birthright in despoiled space seemed an unworthy pursuit. We required only a wordless performative utterance—a *speech(less)* act through which to *shout* Indigenous sovereignty in the fulfillment of an ancient obligation under the setting sun and before the natural world. Within and by means of this ceremonial moment, Maracle deftly demarcated an *edge* between a spiritually despoiled space and a space of power in which to prepare Indigenous minds and bodies to enter colonial space without allowing themselves to be *of* that space.

ESTABLISHING A RHYTHM OF CONCILIATION

JILL: We had begun to establish a rhythm—a rhythm of retreat and then reassembly to re-*treat*,[12] a rhythm of Call and Response. A later chapter in this book, co-authored by nehiyaw deviser-performer Trina Moyan and Euro Canadian deviser-sound designer Shirka Urechko, offers us greater insight into this trope of the "call" and how it influenced the curation of sound within the company's pre-show installation through which the audience moved before finally taking their seats before a proscenium stage. During early discussions in Indigenous space, Trina remarked upon the settler designator for the people of her Nation. There are several accounts of the origin of the word "Cree," including early mispronunciations of a clan-designator or of identifiers offered by other First Nations Peoples during early French exploration, trading, missionization, and settlement (see, for instance, McLeod and Lac Labiche Museum). Trina Moyan offers a different account of the origins of this European designator—an account that has come down to her from nehiyaw language teacher Reuben Quinn. In early company discussions, Trina shared that the word "Cree" finds its origins in the French word for "cry." She spoke of ancient nehiyaw protocols, which include announcing one's approach when overtaking others on a trail, announcing one's presence

12 "Re-treat" is used throughout this book in reference to a history of broken and violated treaties. Without careful and painstaking address and redress of these violations relational repair between Canadians and the Indigenous stewards of these lands is an impossible project. Re-treat here is used to signal the necessity of reassembly to repeat the process of negotiating treaty and/or to begin a new process of treaty-making.

and intentions and awaiting welcome before entering a village, issuing an alarm, and "calling them in" to counsel, feasting, or ceremony. Early French arrivants (explorers, priests, and fur traders) were regularly exposed to an intricate soundscape of coded messages, which they could not comprehend or navigate. Eventually, they began to refer to their nehiyaw hosts as "Les Cris" (see "Cree Calls" later in this book). Here, then, our attempt to flip the script or to break the dam—to set buried waters, buried violence, buried truth free—became our call at the edge of the woods. Through this provocative welcome, we hoped to "call them in" to a territory of uncomfortable truths.

Continuing our work in irreconcilable space, the company began the devising process, deepening its engagement with ancient protocols of Call and Response. With each group of company members, Lee Maracle and her daughter Columpa Bobb called us in with a traditional Stó:lō story mindfully crafted for narration outside of and apart from ceremonial context. Within these initial devising sessions, Lee and Columpa curated an ethical and fluid space in which the company members became, at once, *witnesses* as Lee called us in with story and *witnessed* as each offered a creative response to her challenge / provocation / invitation.

Lee Maracle's storied call[13] chronicles an era of devastation, chaos, and conflict. Assaulted on all sides by fatal visions and catastrophic memories, the human survivors of the Great Flood have no time to bury their dead, to mourn their beloved, or to properly care for the unfathomable numbers of carcasses of other-than-human creatures who in life had sustained their lives. Driven by terror and unaddressed mourning, these survivors

13 The story that Lee Maracle told us sits at the heart of *Encounters at the 'Edge of the Woods.'* It is the foundation upon which this production is based. It is the call to which each creator's story constitutes a response. As Lee would not be able to appear on stage in fall 2019, she directed company member Tash Naveau through the recording and editing of her telling of the story. In performance, a digitized Lee Maracle orates her version of the history of the Double-Headed Serpent in the wake of the Great Flood. The telling has been divided into three sections, which correspond to three directional shifts that occur within *Encounters*. In the script that appears at the end of the book, *only* the first section is transcribed. This is because the audio portion of this first section may be readily accessed, as per Lee Maracle's permission, within a digitally archived land-based truth activation first livestreamed in 2021 (*Streaming Life: Storying the 94*, https://www.youtube.com/watch?v=VxEpi0noKLU). The remainder of Lee's telling is paraphrased through the script you will read here.

begin to turn on each other until their violence awakens greater destruction in the form of a Double-Headed Serpent. This creature of warring impulses attacks and affects the human population, driving the people to increasingly desperate acts. One head "swallows human conscience," perpetuating escalating terror, mistrust, and violence within the human community, while the second head tries to "solve problems," perhaps, by swallowing human terror. After all, as Maracle observed in the telling, "Terrified people can't be trusted." We were not to concentrate on details but to allow the story to "wash over" us. The story became a landscape of sound, image, and memory through which we were encouraged to drift, "Moving," in Dylan Robinson's words, "between layers of positionality" and "listening for our own tin ears" (60). What fear-fueled assumptions did we nurture and what actions did we perpetrate that ran so horribly counter to our good intentions? Who *were* we and how were our stories woven into a centuries-old campaign of genocide on these shores?

"Eventually," Maracle told us, "a small boy said to his mother, 'I'm going to kill that serpent; he's got our people killing each other.'" Ultimately, it is a child who takes it upon himself to put an end to the horror into which he has been born. He embarks upon a perilous journey and encounters the beast that has swallowed the spirits of his relatives, teachers, neighbors, and friends. But here, a beautiful thing happens! The boy finds that repair is possible without further destruction: he is not compelled to kill the serpent and stain his hands with blood. Instead, three heads come together to broker an alliance: the Double-Headed Serpent will leave the people alone. Indeed, it will protect the people! In return, the people will remember to honour the serpent in feasts and ceremonial undertakings. They will remember themselves as human beings. They will remember their ceremonial obligations. And they will conduct themselves accordingly.

BRENDA: At first, I really didn't know what I was going to bring to the play. It was the coaching work of Lee Maracle and Columpa Bobb that created the opening scene for me. As a grandmother, I visualized my grandson, and these are the words that came to me: "His eyes are very familiar. My grandson is very brave. He's always talking about scary things. He has seen this place before." I remember Lee laughing because she could see where these words would fit into the opening scene. She was a genius.

JILL: Each company member responded to Maracle's call by telling the story back (as she instructed) "different but the same." Within the relative safety of irreconcilable space, we were able to articulate our place in the story and to move our truths across the rehearsal space in song, in verse, in fragmented memories. Next, Lee Maracle broke each group (Indigenous and non-Indigenous) into smaller groups. And here, under her guidance, each subgroup engaged in writing exercises through which to interweave the stories of its members.

Below, I offer a fragment of an early weaving session. This piece first emerged as a series of personal responses, which were then interwoven to create the beginnings of a collective response. Eventually, this response re-emerged as a multivocal call issued by the Indigenous cast members to the non-Indigenous cast members within a choral dialogue.

My two brains are spinning, rolling, rolling, spinning inside my skulls
His eyes are very familiar
The serpents are guarding Taddle Creek
My grandson is very brave
Mouths agape; tongues aflame
He's always talking about scary things
Water swallows pain. Cools the nightmare-sweats
He has seen this place before
I am the split-minded serpent rising up from my mother's heart
Petroglyphs.
Asiniin ehahmood.
Kiskinwahamuew Asiniin.
Kinomaagewaapkong.
Sun kisses velvet, watery bed
Mouths agape; tongues aflame
Peering through his magnifying glass
The two-leggeds surrender to the ancient knowledge

Again, we moved these truths across the room, allowing them to take hold of and direct our breathing, our blood flow, our muscles and viscera. Afterwards, the subgroups came back together to create a more intricate and densely layered weave with the material we had generated in our subgroups.

Lee Maracle and Columpa Bobb had rooted us—in blood, bone, and muscle memory—in an ancient teaching about the courage and compassion that must be activated when worlds collapse and terrified humans turn upon each other and upon the rest of Creation with furious, fear-driven hunger. This Double-Headed Serpent that swallows spirit and creates "warriors without conscience" is an eternal being. It lives among us today, just as it did in 2019, in 1867, in 1492, and in every time and every place belonging to the human story. As we found ourselves, in *our* shared time and place, in this ancient story, Maracle told the Indigenous company members, "You are the hub." It was for *us* to issue the call that would draw from the instruments of our non-Indigenous partners an organic response rooted in an eternal present. It was for us to "call them in" and for them to accept or decline the invitation.

When the entire company next met in a shared space of Call and Response, we shared our woven responses and repeated the exercise of first witnessing and then responding to each group's hopes, fears, confessions, experiences, and declarations. As we began to thicken the narrative weave, this space became a liminal zone of encounter in which to address ourselves to the project's central question: How might individuals, estranged by a history of relational violation, begin to build trust in this historical moment?

How might we repair the damage? How might we reintegrate the split mind that engineered the design of Canada? How might we reintegrate the mind that calls out to itself, "Thou shalt not murder; thou shalt not covet; thou shalt not steal" and then responds to its own call with, "The executions of the Indians ought to convince the Red Man that the White Man governs" (Macdonald, qtd. in Hopper)? How might we reawaken to its own humanity the mind that sought to "rescue [Indigenous Peoples] from their barbarity" by spiriting Indigenous children away from their homes and subjecting them to a barbarous re-education program in which starvation, rape, verbal abuse, physical torture, and hard labor were key curricular components (see "10 Quotes")?

BRENDA: Most Canadians are not aware of the damage done to Indigenous Peoples in the 150 years it took to build Canada, especially newcomers who are arriving late to the scene of where we are now as Indigenous Peoples. They see the drunkenness, the beggar, or the ones sleeping on the sidewalk, which in their minds confirms the stereotypes they've been fed even before they arrive here. It will be many years later before they understand what has happened here if they even take the time to learn about it.

In my research for my Doctor of Philosophy I used an arts-based technique called memory mapping. In a sense, I wanted to invite people into my little house, which I have named Nikis, and show them what happened to me and my family. A memory map is a way to locate one's memories onto a map. I mapped out my community and Nikis—my little home—to show the impacts of colonization, racism, and intergenerational violence. My dissertation was informed by showing this map and telling the stories of Nikis to many audiences, mostly here in Toronto and once at an educational conference at Unigraz, Austria.

As I continue to teach Indigenous Studies courses, I continue to tell the story of Nikis. I speak from lived experience, and this has had the most lasting and profound effect on students' understanding of Indigenous issues.

JILL: The personal stories shared in *Encounters at the 'Edge of the Woods'* rest upon a foundational re-creation story given to us by Lee Maracle. They are the beginnings of our re-creation story, as we take stock of the damage in our blasted world, as we wrestle with the serpent that has swallowed the spirits of some and swallowed the conscience of others. As we take back that spirit and conscience, we retreat to the 'Edge of the Woods' where we might encounter each other anew, call to each other (and to our witnesses) in story, and together take up our responsibilities of repair, renewal, re-creation.

BRENDA: Working with the *Encounters* collective has been extremely healing. There's nothing like it when you are so well supported by the group to come out with your story to an audience. I felt that everyone worked so well together, and I would do it again if asked. I am sad for the loss of a great teacher, Lee Maracle. Her vision and her voice will be missed.

JILL: The reflective writings that follow this conversation chronicle the journey of repair undertaken by their authors and testify to what is possible when we remain vigilant, walk softly, and move with care through a process of retreat and re-treating. Accounts from company members and witnesses alike illuminate the experiences of making and of encountering this performative intervention—an intervention that never takes us beyond a place of beginning—beyond the edge of the woods. Within this space of meeting, non-Indigenous colleagues have learned to listen with greater urgency. Here, shared personal truths *offered without equivocation or obfuscation* wind around each other, plaiting themselves into filaments that bind erstwhile strangers into a bittersweet intimacy from which newfound understandings and good intentions might be manifested as effective actions of redress and repair.

The production script that appears at the end of the book constitutes a "snapshot" of a controlled burn—ignited, tended, held, and finally extinguished by a company of "Fire Keepers"[14] who have chosen to scorch the corrupted old-growth of misinformation, miseducation, treachery, and deceit to awaken the deadened Canadian conscience. Our intention throughout this work has been to ignite in Canadians a desire to step forward with their Indigenous neighbors onto this scorched earth out of which the shoots of (k)new[15] life, (k)new imaginings, and (k)new lifeways are already beginning to emerge.

---

14 Here, I reference the remarkable *New Definitions for Indigenous Theatre: Fire Keepers* created for Kimi Clark's "Fire Zine: A *Kamloopa* Study Buddy (see Harvey).

15 I was first introduced to the descriptor "(k)new" by Virginie Magnat, who encountered it in the work of Manulani Aluli-Meyer. Various aspects of Indigenous Knowledge are often "discovered" or adopted by Western scholars who present these as a branch of "new knowledge," regardless of the fact that this knowledge has been known for millennia by Indigenous Peoples. Shane Edwards is credited by Aluli-Meyer for having applied this term to knowledge that is branded as "new" by Western thinkers, although it has been known and applied for millennia by Indigenous Peoples (kinda like "discovering" corn, tobacco, maple syrup, or "America," eh?). The term first appears in Edwards's dissertation *Titiro Whakamuri Kia Marama Ai Te Wao Nei: Whakapapa Epistemologies and Maniapoto Maori Cultural Identities* (see Magnat 24–37, endnote 3).

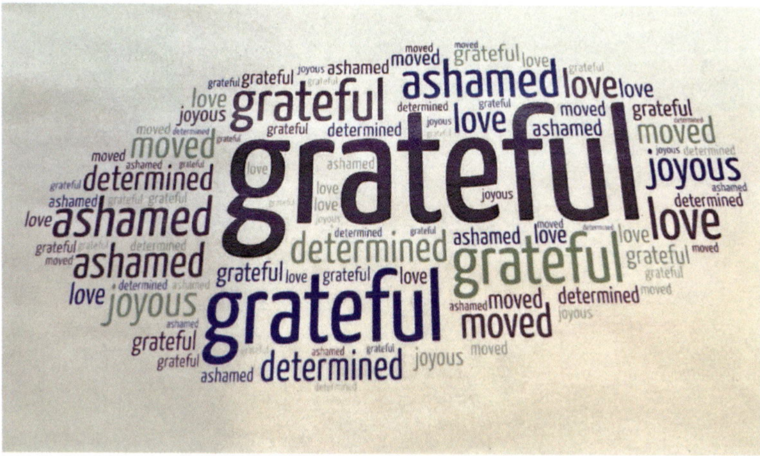

Word cloud gifted to the Collective Encounter. Photo by Jill Carter.

Some weeks after *Encounters* closed, the company was gifted a beautifully framed word cloud by the university administrator who had called me into this project and who had offered considerable supports to ensure its completion. He explained that this was his way of articulating a personal response to the call he had witnessed.

I receive this response as both a testament to the feelings that had been called up in him and an expression of his commitment to act—to exercise the power of his position to institute concrete changes that may go far to contribute to an urgent project of relational repair within these territories. The gift itself performs as a material response to a performative call—a promise yet to be fulfilled. And like the performance to which it responds, it does not signal a happy end or even a satisfactory resolution. Instead, it locates us in an auspicious space of *hopeful beginnings*—a space wherein unreserved acknowledgement and honest conversation might ensue. In this space, the process we have been considering here, the intervention it birthed, and the national project with which these engage remain open—unfinished, like the ends of a wampum belt. In this space of hopeful beginnings, they constitute a tentative call at the edge of a world yet to be rewritten.

WORKS CITED

"10 Quotes John A. Macdonald Made about First Nations." Indigenous Corporate Training Inc. 28 June 2016. https://www.ictinc.ca/blog/10-quotes-john-a.-macdonald-made-about-first-nations.

Arao, Brian, and Kristi Clemens. "From Safe Spaces to Brave Spaces: A New Way to Frame Dialogue around Diversity and Social Justice." In *The Art of Effective Facilitation: Reflections from Social Justice Educators*, edited by Lisa M. Landreman, 135–50. Sterling, VA: Stylus, 2013.

Carter, Jill. "Retreating to Re-Treating from 'Irreconcilable Space': Canadian Theatre Workers and the Project of Conciliation." In *The Directors Lab: Techniques, Methods, and Conversations about All Things Theatre*, edited by Evan Tsitsias, 185–201. Toronto: Playwrights Canada Press, 2019.

Fahs, Breanne. "Reading Between the Lines: Ben Morea on Anarchy, Radicalism, and Revolution." *Quark: Left History*, vol. 16, no. 1 (Spring/Summer 2011): 37–53. https://www.google.com/search?client=firefox-b-d&q=ben+morea+spaxes+of+affinity.

Favel, Floyd. "The Artificial Tree: Native Performance Culture Research 1991–1996." In *Aboriginal Drama and Theatre*, edited by Rob Appleford, 69–73. Critical Perspectives on Canadian Theatre in English, vol. 1. Toronto: Playwrights Canada Press, 2005.

Garneau, David. "Imaginary Spaces of Conciliation and Reconciliation: Art, Curation, and Healing." In *Arts of Engagement: Taking Aesthetic Action in and Beyond the Truth and Reconciliation Commission of Canada*, edited by Keavy Martin, Dylan Robinson, David Garneau, et. al., 21–41. Waterloo: Wilfred Laurier Press, 2016.

Hart House. "About Us. Hart House Since 1919." https://harthouse.ca/about/history.

Harvey, Kim Senklip. *Kamloopa: An Indigenous Matriarch Story.* Vancouver: Talonbooks, 2020.

Hopper, Tristan. "Here is What Sir John A. Macdonald did to Indigenous People." *National Post.* 28 August 2018. https://nationalpost.com/news/canada/here-is-what-sir-john-a-macdonald-did-to-indigenous-people.

King, Thomas. *The Truth About Stories: A Native Narrative.* Toronto: House of Anansi Press, 2003.

Lac Labiche Museum. "Regional Cultures: Cree." Nehiyawak Archives. 6 April 2017. https://laclabichemuseum.com/tag/nehiyawak/.

Magnat, Virginie. "(K)new Materialisms: Honouring Indigenous Perspectives." *Theatre Research in Canada* 43, no. 1 (2022): 24–37.

McLeod, Neal. "Cree." In *Indigenous Saskatchewan Encyclopedia.* University of Saskatchewan. https://teaching.usask.ca/indigenoussk/import/cree.php.

Nolan, Yvette. *Medicine Shows: Indigenous Performance Culture.* Toronto: Playwrights Canada Press, 2015.

Poll, Melissa. "Towards an Eighth Fire Approach: Developing Modes of Indigenous-Settler Performance-Making on Turtle Island." *Contemporary Theatre Review*, vol. 31, no. 4. (July 2021): 390–408. https://doi.org/10.1080/10486801.2021.1969556.

Robinson, Dylan. *Hungry Listening: Resonant Theory for Indigenous Sound Studies.* Minneapolis: U of Minnesota P, 2020.

Vizenor, Gerald. *Manifest Manners: Narratives on Postindian Survivance.* Lincoln: U of Nebraska P, 1994.

Wastasecoot, Brenda I. "Showing and Telling the Story of Nikis (My Little House): An Arts-Based Autoethnographic Journey of a Cree Adult Educator." Doctoral dissertation. University of Toronto, 2017. https://tspace.library.utoronto.ca/bitstream/1807/82394/3/Wastasecoot_Brenda_I_201706_PhD_thesis.pdf.

Yazzie, Rhiana. "Digging Deep with Native Theatre Icon Muriel Miguel." *American Theatre*. 11 July 2022. https://www.americantheatre.org/2022/07/11/digging-deep-with-native-theatre-icon-muriel-miguel/.

Cree Calls

SHIRKA URECHKO IN CONVERSATION WITH TRINA MOYAN

While doing research for this chapter, I came across a land acknowledgement provided online for the Flin Flon School Division by the Manitoba Association of Parent Councils (MAPC) in affiliation with The Manitoba Teachers' Society. It reads, "The Flin Flon School Division operates on the traditional land of the Ininew people. The Flin Flon School Division respects the Treaties that were made on this territory" in English, French, and Cree in that order (Manitoba Association). Upon further investigation I found posted on the website of the Flin Flon School Division another land acknowledgement: "We acknowledge that we are signatories of Treaty Five and that we reside in the traditional territory of the Cree Nation and the Metis People. We are all Treaty people," which is echoed on the Facebook page of my elementary and junior high school now known as École McIsaac School (Flin Flon).

I was born in Flin Flon, Manitoba, in 1974 and lived there until I was fourteen years of age. My father's side of the family is Ukrainian, and my mother's side is English but, as a child, I did not know I was a Ukrainian English Canadian settler occupying Cree territory in adherence to Treaty 5. The English side of my family did not interest me as much as the Ukrainian side. After all, I spoke English and grew up on land colonized by English settlers, so once I had satiated myself with castles, queens, princesses, and my grandparents' accents, there wasn't much more that held my attention. The Ukrainian side was mysterious due to the language I heard often but did not understand except for a word or a phrase here and there. There were secrets in those sounds, and they created powerful divisions in our family. I wanted to know what was happening, but the only way in was through those words and, for me, the door was locked.

My grandpa told me that when he was a young man during the early 1940s, he rode the boxcars from his home in a small farming hamlet within the Ukrainian diaspora on the prairies of southern Saskatchewan to find work up north in the mines of Flin Flon. I wonder what this hopeful young man thought as golden fields gave way to rocky lakes and dense forests as he sped north, deep into the Canadian Shield so full of life. When I think about my grandpa's journey, I am reminded of Cree activist and writer Clayton Thomas-Müller's description of the trains in his memoir, *Life in the City of Dirty Water*:

> For many Native people, the train is a power archetype, the Iron Horse. Trains brought with them colonial expansion. Each train brought more white people. The train says, "Hey get out of the way!" When the track-laying crews arrived, those spikes might as well have been pounded into our hearts. That steel ribbon cut us off from our own past. So the train is burned into every Indian's psyche . . . With colonization, trains replaced the rivers which were the life vein of transportation and an essential food source. Our rivers in the north were all dammed. It was the trains that brought food, trains that brought loved ones home. Trains took our people away, and sometimes trains brought them home. (171–72)

Although my grandpa was born in Canada, I imagine he was leaving land similar to his ancestral home in Ukraine when he left the prairies of Saskatchewan. It can be argued the Iron Horse brought my grandpa to a place that was foreign from a land that was also not his own. My father was born in Flin Flon because the trains carried my grandparents there. The tracks ran parallel to my street growing up, and like many kids I was drawn to the trains. I waved to the engineers honking their horns as they passed and followed their tracks through the trees.

There is something in the blood and bones that recognizes home. When I lived in Northern Manitoba, I carried a nagging sense of displacement within me that I couldn't put my finger on and could never quite shake. Not every Canadian feels this way, of course, but I suspect a sense of "not belonging" within those whose lineage extends through generations of settlers is more prevalent than we, as a society, may realize. To me, being "Canadian" always seemed a vague, rootless, and inaccurate idea—especially as a child trying to discover who I was and wanted to be. When my family moved south to the prairies, I immediately felt like I was home. The vast expanses of land and huge sky were a comfort and a joy from the start. Once freed from the confines of rocks, lakes, and forests, I finally felt like myself.

My identity as a Canadian is something I would only come to formally interrogate when I began my education in Indigenous studies at the University of Toronto. Dismantling the version of history I was taught both in and outside of public school was an experience that I found profoundly unsettling and deeply disturbing. In fact, *colonizer* is a word I did not hear until the age of forty, and I met my identity as a settler with a lot of resistance at first. A large part of the difficulty of digesting the concept of not belonging the way I thought I did to somewhere I was born was precisely because of how thoroughly it flipped the script I was taught in public school by those whose authority I believed I could trust. I did not yet understand the education system to be in service of a colonial state. Eventually, I accepted my settler identity as truth and realized my feeling of displacement may somehow be connected to this. I was encouraged by some of my professors to explore my own indigeneity as a settler, so I began to trace back my steps. In the beginning there was Flin Flon, my family, and the Ukrainian language that neither my father nor my brother nor I were encouraged to speak lest it interfere with "our English." I learned that language is important. It's better to erase the past to make way for the future. Such was the wisdom of the time.

I have fond memories of McIsaac School as it was known back in the mid-1970s and '80s. The school sat alongside a beautiful creek, and there was a big hill to toboggan down beside the Joe Brain Petting Zoo, where deer would gaze at us from behind a fence with their soft and gentle brown eyes. Many a bone was broken on that hill and many giggles bounced off the snow. Inside, tucked away in the library, a wonderful librarian read stories to us with her rich and sonorous voice. The scent of cookies baking in the home economics room drifted sweetly to us from down the hall. We made pickled eggs in science class and covered the jungle gym like monkeys at recess. It was a great school. However, any acknowledgement of Indigenous Peoples was not a part of the school board's mandate or school curriculum during that time. I knew the words Cree and Métis but did not know Indigenous languages were still spoken where I lived. I did not know about ininew, the Peter Ballantyne Cree Nation, or that I was attending school with some of the children of their communities. I was, however, fascinated by stories of birch-bark canoes, pemmican, wigwams, fur trading, totem poles, and igloos told by my teachers, all of whom appeared to be white. I learned about Indigenous

Peoples past and present as they were viewed through the distorted lens of colonization. From this perspective, the Canadian government *gave* Indigenous Peoples land in the form of reserves. Treaties were presented as amicable agreements made by two parties entirely of their own free will for the benefit of all. At least, this is what I recall, and that is what I retained. What I do know is that the truth of coercion and genocide was not revealed to me in school, in church, or in my daily life at any point during that time.

After a few years of study and personal reflection, I know more than I did as a child growing up in Northern Manitoba. I understand I am a settler sustaining myself on Indigenous territory and that I share a responsibility to uphold the agreements contained in Treaty 13 in addition to those specified by the Williams Treaties in the Greater Toronto Area where I currently reside. I do my best to respect the Dish With One Spoon treaty, which covers territory that is home to the Mississaugas of the Credit, the Anishinaabe, the Haudenosaunee, as well as other First Nations, the Métis and Inuit, in addition to settlers and newcomers from other lands. I make efforts toward learning to respect and care for the land itself from those who have been its stewards for thousands of years. I acknowledge that these lands were taken illegally through trickery and force and the truth that we are all here now and need to work together to rectify the situation.

Land acknowledgements are considered by many to be empty token gestures because there has been so little movement toward answering the ninety-four calls to action put forth by the Truth and Reconciliation Commission of Canada in 2015. While this failure to act with the urgency that is called for cannot be denied, land acknowledgements do serve a purpose. The fact that they are now widespread means they disseminate important information to Canadian society and keep the presence of Indigenous Peoples within our collective conscience. Everyone now has access to the true history of Canada and the genocide that continues to be uncovered (Truth and Reconciliation Commission). It is the collective responsibility of settlers on Indigenous territory to redress its ongoing effects and learn more about the strength, resilience, and cultures of the people upon whose lands we occupy. It is in this spirit that I asked Cree multidisciplinary artist Trina Moyan if she would allow me to interview her on the subject of Cree calls.

Trina Moyan is nehiyaw iskwew (Plains Cree) from the Frog Lake First Nation in Northern Alberta, Treaty 6 Medicine Chest territory, and she is one of the most captivating people I have ever met. She is a riveting storyteller, and it was no surprise to anyone that she blossomed in her first theatrical role for *Encounters at the 'Edge of the Woods,'* under the direction of Jill Carter. As a member of the sound design team, I had been listening for ways in which we could incorporate the stories performers were telling into the realm of audio. I was moved by all that they shared but found Cree artist Brenda Wastasecoot's story from her childhood in Northern Manitoba and what the trains meant to her particularly striking. I decided to weave the voice of trains into a pre-performance sound installation to illustrate her story and those of so many others. When I happened upon Trina practising Cree calls outside of rehearsal, I was struck by their beauty and asked for her permission to thread them in and around the trains. The effect was mesmerizing and I was curious to learn about what Cree calls mean to Trina personally, about the place they hold in her culture, and their connection to the land where I grew up. The following conversation has been edited for length and clarity.

SHIRKA: Can you tell me what Cree calls are? I'm interested in the history of the name Cree because I have heard you mention this was not a true name but a renaming by settlers.

TRINA: Yes. So, Reuben Quinn is a Cree language teacher at The Centre for Race and Culture in Edmonton, Alberta, and he tells this fantastic story. For the most part, Europeans decided to come up with their own exonyms when they encountered us—renaming us, essentially. In French "la cri" means "the cry." When our people, the nehiyawak, saw the European ships on the St. Lawrence River, these gigantic ships, we called out in awe and in warning to give each other the information that there were newcomers entering our lands.

Once we got to know the French, they learned that we're very noisy, or at least that was how they decided to describe us. But calling amongst the Cree and for many other First Nations and Indigenous groups has always been essential to survival and a way to communicate with each other across open spaces. The French decided to call us la Cri. When we encountered them for trade, they would say, "la Cri are here." That's how we ended up with that exonym; eventually it became Cree, but we never called ourselves that.

We were always the nehiyawak, which mean the "four-bodied" or the "four-spirited" people and is based on the number four. In nehiyawewin, our language, we count peyak (one), niso (two), nisto (three), newo (four). And it is the number four that we based our name on—nehiyawak—the four-bodied or the spirited or four-centred people. That's where we centre ourselves in the circle because we know the four is sacred. We honour the four cardinal directions, the four stages of life, the four medicines, the four elements. When we look at the world around us, we can see life within fours. There is much more of course. Beyond that there's the sphere, the sky energy, the earth energy, and so on. There is something else floating in space—that energy that keeps us together, making connections to the metaphysical. We know the four directions hold us to that "other" power, to that presence, to the great mystery. Reuben talks about that and so do my parents. I'm speaking also about the way my parents talk about our existence and our place.

That's a part of being "the people that call out." I thought it was interesting because the French recognized that we call, that we are callers; we're always calling and seeking the response—the call and the response of life. As much as I don't like the fact that they gave us the exonym, it still carries that meaning. And the French were our friends, right? At least for a time. We had allied ourselves with them. So, I like the idea that they called us "the people that called out" because it's so true: we call to centre ourselves and to align with the metaphysical world and the power of the "other."

SHIRKA: So, just to make sure I'm understanding you; Cree calls were a part of the culture long before French settlers arrived and the true name of Cree people is nehiyawak, not Cree, correct?

TRINA: No, actually that name it is specifically the Plains Cree language with the "Y" dialect: nehiyawak. There is the "N" dialect and the "th" dialect and there are many different dialects based upon the uniqueness of Cree communities. In different areas there are many dialects of Cree. There are the Woods Cree and the Swampy Cree and Oji-Cree and so on.

SHIRKA: Okay.

TRINA: Being a true human being is really what being nehiyawak is, or at least that is the goal. To be balanced within those four sacred directions. I'm certainly not an expert about other Indigenous groups, but what many groups call themselves is either "the real human beings" or "the true human beings." We refer to ourselves as the true human beings. Many Indigenous Nations do that, and this is again a calling, right? It's what we are supposed to be trying to do. It's the goal. You're calling to yourself to live up to that concept, to be the truest person you can be, to be in balance within the four directions and the four corners, honouring all of life and knowing that you're just one little facet of it. That's how you can become that true being, by making sure you're honouring, recognizing, and respecting all of that.

Anyway, my parents speak in that way about themselves and our people. Cree calling is what you hear and respond to, but there is also that calling to yourself and to the rest of the community. Because if you say you're a nehiyawak person, then how are you demonstrating that in your life? So, there is the literal calling, the everyday calling that you do, and then there is that deeper calling within yourself, and we talked about this with Jill for *Encounters at the 'Edge of the Woods.'* Specifically, we talked about this in relation to the Haudenosaunee people, the Mohawk people, and the Six Nations, but almost all Indigenous groups have these calls. We just happened to be called by the French "la Cri," the noisiest of them all, and yes, I suppose we are noisy—the Cree!

The idea of the encounter at the edge of the woods is that concept or that practice, the protocols of engagement, of respect and safety when you're in territory that is not yours. You call out to let those who live there know you're there because you don't know if they're going to attack you or welcome you. That's safety and it's the respect. Also, when you are calling in general, when you walk through the forest, when you walk through the woods, you call because you want to show respect to all of the animal beings there. You call to the babies and the mommies because you don't want to startle them. You call out to give them warning so that they can take cover or move and you're also calling so that animals won't attack you. You don't want to startle a bear. It's just common sense. You're calling as you travel through. You're calling out to those who are there, to allow yourself to be known, and to announce your presence because it's a part of respect and safety.

In all civilizations throughout the world, there is the other facet of calling in spiritual way, like the Call and Response in songs. In so many of those beautiful Haudenosaunee songs and dances, there's that Call and Response. They have many different dances, but for one dance—it's something like the Round Dance—within that movement, that shuffle movement, there's a caller who calls out in vocables or in the language. I'm not Haudenosaunee, but I remember learning with Professor Amos Key the Call and Response during that dance. What that does is it creates a bond in the community that demonstrates you're on the same page, that you're in this together, sharing that spirit, that energy, and the moment. It's a celebration and way to reinforce connection to one another. You can liken it to when you go to a concert and you're all of the same mind, you're all of the same energy, and you're all moving with that motion, that wave of energy. You're connected that way. That's why we like to go to concerts, not only to listen to the music but to be connected.

If you think about what's happened here with COVID-19, so many people talk about missing that collective energy, whether it's going to a concert or any other kind of social gathering. My family and I went to *Jesus Christ Superstar* the other night, and all three of us commented on how nice it is to sit in the theater and to be one because we're all having a shared experience and that oneness is there. That's what community is. That Call and Response is a part of that. You want a response, and you want to feel them answer you with their energy. It's like when you text somebody or you email them: you hope to get a response. You wait for it and hope for it. And it feels good to receive it.

SHIRKA: This reminds me of the Anglican Church services that I grew up going to. In church, when the minister says something, the congregation calls back.

TRINA: And they respond, there you go. Same thing. It's the same sort of spiritual connection. You need to respond to the call. In today's cyber world it feels terrible to be ghosted, but that is also an answer.

SHIRKA: It seems to be a universal human need to have a Call and Response.

TRINA: Oh, yeah, for sure. You've probably seen it also in the movies. They'll send out a scout to mark a path and make sure the way is safe. When the scout gets to a certain measure of the land, he knows that his call can only be heard from so much a distance, so at that point, he calls out to let the community—the people—know that the way is either safe or not safe. Various kinds of sounds and calls are used, and a lot of them are mimicking the sound of birds and animals. I mean, it's like when my uncles go hunting in the fall, there are calls specifically to the moose or to the ducks.

SHIRKA: When I was young and living up north, my grandpa showed me how he called to the moose and ducks by mimicking their sounds when he was hunting. I think settlers like him must have learned this from the Indigenous Peoples whose hunting grounds they were on because moose don't exist on the prairies where he came from.

TRINA: Yes, and when you are hunting and call to the animals, you're waiting for that response so that you can go and harvest that animal. So, there are various kinds of calls like that to let the community know that they can go forward or stay back.

SHIRKA: So, are there other instances when the community responds as a group outside of relaying information about safety?

TRINA: Yes, and this is interesting. For example, we say "ayhay" or "hayhay." You've probably heard this, especially with the Cree. People spell it in different ways, and the roman orthography is used to get the sound across to English speakers. There have been various understandings of what that word means, but for me, growing up and in my community with my parents, you would always hear it. If you're given something or if there's someone speaking, you'll see the people collectively say "ayhay" or "hiy hiy." Over time, it's being used more commonly as a way to say thank you. Most people think it means thank you. I asked my parents about that, and my mother, who is now seventy-six and was raised very traditionally, explained what that word really means. She said that it's what the old people always said when the community came together to meet and make decisions. When the speaker was saying their words, it was disrespectful to not vocalize that you're either in agreement or you're just respecting what that person is saying and acknowledging their energy. So again, it's the Call and Response. When the person would speak, during the discussion, throughout the talk, the people, the Elders, especially, would go "mhm, aha, ayhai, hayhay" and eventually it became "hayay," "ayhay," or "hiy hiy."

My mom said that, over time, it evolved, and this is what the Cree people say. They say, "ayhay" to say, "I heard you" or "I respect what you said" or "I'm in agreement with you." It can also mean "thank you." But this, again, is a traditional Cree protocol. If you go to a Cree event, you'll notice they'll always go "mhm" in response to the person speaking. They don't just sit there silently staring at the speaker. They're always in an active relationship. And that energy is always supposed to be shared. So that's a part of that calling, that call and the response, "ayhay." So that person feels heard. So that person doesn't feel alone, as though no one has heard them.

Doesn't it feel weird when you're speaking, especially in Zoom calls these days, and there's no response. It's just silent screens. And often people won't even put their video on and you're just talking to blankness. That's just not natural, right? It doesn't feel natural. And Cree people are very interactive. We're always wanting to have that constant flow of energy between one another. We're renowned for being people of love. Our number one law is wâhkôhtowin—meaning to have love for our relations. That's why there's so many of us—we're lovers! We're the largest Indigenous Nation in Canada. Cree are the most populous, so you'll find us from coast to coast. The Cree are everywhere across this country, and this is because we are relationship people. We are also matriarchal societies.

When I think of growing up, I remember berry picking with my nokum (grandmother). Even when sitting there silently, you're always communicating with the people you're berry picking with because you don't want to lose each other, right, so you'll go "*ah*." Sounds funny, but theirs is always a little call, and you know that kokum is over there somewhere. You can't see her, but she'll call out every now and again and then you call back to make sure everybody is still in the same vicinity. If you get silence, uh-oh, somebody's either in trouble or lost, so I've got to go find them, and that's for safety, for taking care of each other.

I was thinking about music, and you know this with your own musical background: music is written in either four bars or eight bars or sixteen bars, and in music there is also a call at the end of the bar, right [*Trina sings*]. Then the next four bars will answer it and finish the melody [*Trina sings*].

SHIRKA: Yeah, yeah.

TRINA: It's the same structure in our songs. There's the Call and Response to all of the vocables, and you'll hear it in the big drums and the hand drum songs. At the Pow Wow that you attended I'm sure you stood, and you watched, and you were listening. There's a lead singer calling in the vocables, and then the rest of the singers answer, and it's done in four rounds. Each song is done in the four rounds, and there's always that completion of the music, but it's not a drum song unless there's a response to the main singer. It's the same with the hand drum songs. You'll have a group of men or women hand drumming, and there will be the lead hand drummer who will create the beat and the melody and then he'll call and everybody else will respond. That's the same with all of the ceremonial songs where you'll really hear the Cree language, and those are so beautiful because they are only for ceremony. They're not for public consumption. There are the rattle songs and the drum songs, and you'll only hear those specific songs in the sweat lodge or in the Sun Dance lodge. There are many other nations and there are different lodges.

Again, what's essential when you're in the Sweat is the calling that takes place. It will either be the men's side that will do the calling and the women will respond or vice versa. It's powerful and it's beautiful. There is also the Shaking Tent ceremony where you're calling to the Spirits, and they come in. I have not had that personal experience because I've always been a little afraid, but my mom and dad speak of being in those ceremonies where you keep calling, and you have to keep calling to receive the response. It's a powerful interchange. Eventually it's so powerful that you call in the Eagle Spirit or whichever Spirit that the conductor intends to call in. My mom spoke of how the Eagle Spirit landed on her shoulder.

She said it was so heavy, and she felt it's talons digging into her shoulder: she received the response from the Eagle Spirit.

SHIRKA: Whoa.

TRINA: My whole family practiced the Shaking Tent, and many still do—where there would be a transference of human beings that are not even within the ceremony that are brought in either for discipline or for some other reason. It's all based on the calling. That constant repetition of the song. The call and the collective energy is so powerful that you can actually bring in a human being and bring in those Spirits. My mom and dad talked about the rumbling. They were having a Shaking Tent ceremony in a basement and my mom said she was so scared because the whole house started to rumble. What they had called in together was the Bigfoot Spirit, the Sasquatch, and that Spirit entered the space. That's the power of calling, and I think that's the metaphysical aspect that we're missing today. I know my family, when we really tap into reaching out, to calling out to one another, we tap into the unknown, what is referred to as the sixth sense.

Largely, humanity is cut off from one another because we're only tapping into our taste and our smell and our touch or sight, but there is that other sense. We were once far more connected to each other, and we could share that energy. That's calling where nothing is said. So, you might call it the sixth sense today, but it's in the solar plexus. What we call intuition, and for my family, when I really sit with it, and I really think about it, and I dwell on it, and I pray on it, and I release myself from being held to the material world I can feel my parents and they can feel me. They'll always know if there's something wrong with me. They'll phone me up and they'll say, "Trina, what's going on? Your dad and I dreamt of you," or "your dad had a feeling that you're not okay." And they're always right. Either there is something wrong or I'm sick. It's in the reverse as well. If I'm really thinking about my parents, I will know, "Oh, something's up, I've got to call Mom and Dad." I'm sure you've had that experience too.

SHIRKA: Yeah. It's interesting because while we've been sitting here talking about language, my brother texted me about our language, or our grandparents' language, and asked me a question about something that our grandpa used to say to us in Ukrainian. I often have experiences like this with my family and certain close friends.

TRINA: Right.

SHIRKA: So, yeah, there's a connection.

TRINA: Yeah, for sure. Sylvia McAdam Saysewahum has videos posted about those kinds of stories (McAdam). In her family, she talks about how there was always that other connection, that much deeper connection to the great mystery. When we were closer to the natural world, living in and amongst the animals and other beings, we had a much deeper, natural connection to the earth, to the land, to the plant beings; that's where the magic was, but because we've been so severed from all of that, most of us have lost that ability. That's another reason why, when you look at therapy for young people in urban centres, the best programs are always the ones in the wilderness and on the land. Go climb in the mountains, go to the horse ranch and spend time on the land. Those are the best programs to heal because you're healing the spirit and you're recreating those severed connections and we always feel better, don't we? So that's all a part of the calling.

SHIRKA: Yes. I found a lot of healing hitchhiking and living outside in the Okanogan Valley when I was young. Obviously, I'm lucky I'm alive, and I know that now, but at the time, living outside did something very good for me. I think I was the healthiest I've ever been physically during that time, and it certainly did a lot for my mental health as well. Now that I think about it, when I look back on my life, a lot of the healing I have experienced is associated with land. Even now, I live across from the beach and I find healing from the lake because I experienced a lot of loss and change as many of us did during the pandemic. Every day, the lake is in a different mood, like all of us. Sometimes it's calm, sometimes it's rough, and there's everything in between, of course, and this is expressed through the sound and motion of the water.

TRINA: Totally.

SHIRKA: How central would you say the calls are to nehiyaw culture? It sounds to me like they are a fundamental part of the culture. Do you think this is true?

TRINA: Yeah, I think you've probably just described it. It's fundamental. It is fundamental along with the actual vocalization in terms of what we already talked about: the hunting, entering territory, coming home, moving, leading the community, the calling, the safety, the respect, all of that, but then there's the calling with no sound. I think that's the bigger, more important calling for my own people, I would say. I'm a Sun Dancer and when you're in the sacred spaces, you're completely silent, you're only dancing and looking at the King Tree. You do that for three days and there is no sound. You don't say anything. You're not allowed to look away from the tree. You're looking only at that tree for three days, and you're dancing to the drummers drumming those sacred songs. If you're seen looking away from the King Tree, you're reminded to look back. They'll come and they'll tap you with the stick, but there's nothing said. So, it's very fascinating, and what you're doing is calling spiritually, for healing for and from the sun because we honour the sun, and through the Sun Dance and that King Tree, we know it reaches up to the sun and it gives life to the earth. We recognized and honour where we come from because we know we are Star People, that our first home is there in the universe amongst those celestial beings.

So, yes. If I'm answering the question, it's essential to our ceremonies. It's just as essential in everyday life. It's essential when you're sitting with community. It's essential to respond when someone's speaking to you, when someone's speaking to the community, so I would say that it's everything. It's all those things. It's the metaphysical, it's the physical, it's the emotional, it's the psychological. Is this making sense?

SHIRKA: Yes, definitely. It's amazing. I've learned so much today listening to you speak and I want to say thank you in your language. Can you tell me again?

TRINA: All you have to do is just say "aha" and eventually, if you were sitting with Cree people or listening to someone or an Elder, you would say "mhm," "aha," "ayhay," "hiy hiy." That's the other part of the language, too.

Everything in the language is active and everything is animate. There is no inanimate and animate. Everything has life. So when you're speaking the language, the description, once translated, is so lovely and so expressive and so alive that when you're just speaking the language, there's the speaking of it, but then you're also calling out to everything you're talking about. You're describing it. You're honouring it. You can speak a language like English, but I'm not honouring everything within each word when I speak it.

In nehiyawewin, you are honouring everything. Every word is like a celebration of the energy of what you're talking about, and it's just beautiful. Embedded within the words of the language is a calling out to all of life. Anytime she was speaking, my nokum would always hold a grandfather rock or her sweetgrass or something of the earth, because she knew that that was all of life and that we're all connected to it. The calling out and speaking is connected to that very rock.

SHIRKA: I took Professor Ryan Decaire's Kanien'kéha (Mohawk language) class at the University of Toronto, and he talked a lot about how the language is verb-based. Nothing is dead in the language. Everything is animate, even something like this table.

TRINA: This is still alive.

SHIRKA: I've heard people say even a computer is alive because it's made of elements.

TRINA: Yeah. It's made of everything. Everything is of the earth.

SHIRKA: The Kenien'kéha greeting, shé:kon, skennen'kó:wa ken?, I've been told translates to "hello, is there great peace?"

TRINA: It's like, "How is your spirit?" When you're saying "hello" you're actually asking not "How are you?" but "How is your spirit?"

SHIRKA: Yeah, whereas in English we just say "hi." It means nothing other than a greeting.

TRINA: It's a word, right.

SHIRKA: But what does it mean? Nothing, really.

TRINA: Exactly. Yesterday I was talking to my mom, and she was reminding me how to properly honour the four corners because I carry my Sun Dance bundle and I have to smudge it at least once a week. I have to pray with it at least once a week, and when you pray, you've got to connect and mean it from the heart. I said to her, "Oh, Mom, I was praying with my bundle, and I don't think I remember how to say the four corners properly," so she went through it with me again. The East, sâkâstenohk—"Mom, the translation?" And she said, "Okay, now you're standing to the east where that angel sits as protection, and you are truly saying this is where life begins in the east where the sun shines." Every direction has a deeper meaning. She reminded me that when you are calling out to that eastern energy, that eastern presence, that power, that spirit, understand that that's what you're doing—calling the Spirit. What is the response that you get? You might not hear anything, but you can feel it. If you meant it when you called out and if you go around that circle and if your spirit is really centred there, you can feel those energies respond, but you have to allow yourself to let go and focus all of your power there.

Deep scientific understanding of the world around us can happen by just sitting and observing and being one with it. Sylvia McAdam tells a fantastic story about how deeply connected to that power and that magic we used to be as beings on the Earth. Her grandfather, her grandmother, or her great grandmother—I can't remember exactly—but they had these needles that they received from the Europeans. They were beading because they were selling their work for money, but they ran out of needles, so her husband took porcupine quills and laid them in his hands. He prayed and he prayed and he prayed, and he had such a power and connection to the natural environment and its magic that when he opened his hands, there were steel needles in them that the women were able to use.

We talk about these stories. Lee Maracle talked about shapeshifters. My great, great grandfather would talk to the Bear, shapeshift, and become one with the Bear. Think about that. These stories don't come from nowhere.

There is one other thing I wanted to mention. This one is a little controversial, but when we look at what's happening right now, like with Joseph

Boyden, Michelle Latimer, and now Dr. Carrie Bourassa, these people are in the news. They have all claimed to be Indigenous—Métis, specifically—because with mixed blood it's easy to look non-Indigenous but claim that you are Indigenous. They've called out, "We're Indigenous," and they're claiming this publicly. They are taking positions as People and have nice careers because of it and have won awards and scholarships because of it, etc., etc. They have wonderful jobs, well-paying jobs, but the idea there is that once they were questioned—"Are you actually Indigenous? Where is the proof?"—by the communities they claimed to be a part of, there was no evidence. So, there was that kind of collective call out to the Indigenous community, but the community did not respond. That's why Joseph Boyden and Michelle Latimer are no longer in the community and now Carrie Bourassa, and there are many, many others.

That's the other aspect of respecting community, respecting nations. If you are claiming and calling out that you're something you're not, or if you are claiming and calling out that you are something. If the community doesn't respond to confirm it than you have also received your answer. This is another aspect of the call—you need the response.

SHIRKA: Right.

TRINA: Yeah. And I mean, I'm not here to judge, but all you have to do is look at the larger picture, because no community has claimed these people as their own. That being said, there's a whole other aspect there about adoption.

I had to talk with my mom and dad about non-Indigenous people claiming to be Indigenous. They said they had mercy. We should have mercy for those ones, because if they were nehiyawak, true human beings, if they were centred with themselves, they wouldn't be needing to claim to be something they're not. They're these lost souls. We should have mercy on them because they're lost. They don't know who they are. They don't really know where they're from, but they're taking what they need. They're taking it without calling out to the community first to ask permission—that's the problem.

My mom and dad talked about this man who had just passed away, a blond, blue-eyed, beautiful Cree-speaking person, a true nehiyawak man. They talked about him, and they mourned him, and we cried on the phone together. I was asking them questions about him, and they said, "Well, he was a true nehiyawak." I said "Really? Why?" They explained that he was a white boy whose parents died when he was a baby, and he was adopted by a Cree family on the reserve where he was raised up as a nehiyawak. He became the most beloved Medicine Man, ceremonial man, Cree-speaking man, and was just a gem to the community but his bloodlines had no Cree.

So, there's the other side to that, right? If somebody says, "I just don't know who I am, and I can't find bloodlines or my history or any of my ancestors, but I'd like to come live amongst your people and truly live a true life with you," if that's the case, then they really can become a nehiyawak person—with respect. They are embedded in the community, and this becomes the fabric of who they are. Then they would be called nehiyawak. Many white women who married native men and received Status moved to the reserve and lived their lives there. They became nehiyawak women—white women, but still the community accepted them.

The number one law for the nehiyawak people is wâhkôhtowin which is "to love," to love all my relationships. That's the number one law. And if you can't practice that, and if you can't call out in love, then you are missing the meaning of being that full, four-bodied person. That applies also to these people who are claiming to be Indigenous. First, let's approach it and love. Let's find out what's wrong with them. Let's try to help them. Let's not just hate them and cancel them. That's not nice either. Let's sit and talk to them and say, "Well, so what happened? How are you feeling? And what made you decide one day to start saying you're Indigenous? Oh, this is where you went wrong. Well, maybe we can help you fix that so you feel better about yourself. Maybe we can help guide you to your own people."

SHIRKA: I feel a lot better personally after this conversation today. Listening to you has helped me deal with some of the stuff I've been thinking about lately when it comes to my own culture and identity.

TRINA: That's the thing. We're all human beings. We're all just human beings. John Kim Bell was talking about Leonard Bernstein, the great conductor. What he recognized in his study of music and language is that no matter where on this beautiful planet we are, we all start with the same sound, "ma-ma." All languages start with that sound. We're all connected. I like to think that connection through "ma-ma," even our songs, you know that "mmm" sound is paying respect to what we call Mother Earth, mama, mother, nemama, nikawiy in Cree. That sound connects. It's a universal language, and we all are speaking the same language. It just depends on how connected or disconnected we are from the environment—a natural environment. It's hard to connect to that in the city. That's why I carry a rock around in my pocket.

SHIRKA: I'm not doing that, but maybe I will.

TRINA: Do! Why not?

SHIRKA: *Aha*, Trina. Thank you.

I deeply appreciate Trina's generosity in sharing her knowledge of Cree calls, how they radiate to other aspects of her culture, and how this, in turn, relates to my own experience living as a settler on Indigenous territory. Her words echo those of the great Cree writer, Harold R. Johnson, in his brilliant book, *The Power of Story: On Truth the Trickster, and New Fictions for a New Era*:

> I am told to call the settler people kiciwamanawak. It means "our cousins" . . . All of us sitting around the fire this evening are family. We are related. None of us has a superior right to be here. We can make up stories about sovereignty, about land ownership—but they are just stories. Only the worms know the truth, and they are waiting for us regardless of which story we choose to tell ourselves. Eventually we are all going to belong to this land. (63)

WORKS CITED

Flin Flon School Division. "Land Acknowledgement." 21 January 2023. https://www.ffsd.mb.ca/home.

Johnson, Harold R. *The Power of Story: On Truth the Trickster, and New Fictions for a New Era*. Windsor: Biblioasis, 2022.

Manitoba Association of Parent Councils. "Acknowledging the Traditional Lands of the Indigenous Peoples of Manitoba." November 2018. https://mapc.mb.ca/resources/indigenous-education.

McAdam, Sylvia. *Cree Teachings*. YouTube. 2023. https://www.youtube.com/@sylviamcadam-creeteachings3205/videos.

Thomas-Müller, Clayton. *Life in The City of Dirty Water: A Memoir of Healing*. Toronto: Penguin Random House Canada, 2021.

Truth and Reconciliation Commission of Canada. *Final Report of The Truth And Reconciliation Commission of Canada: Summary, Honouring the Truth, Reconciling for The Future.* Vol. 1. Toronto: James Lorimer & Company, 2015.

Calling All acakos iskwewak (Star Women) to the Edge of kikawinaw askiy (Mother Earth)

TRINA MOYAN

CALL

"Cree Woman's Song: Iskwewuk"

Iskwewuk waniskak! (Women, wake up)
Iskwewuk waniskak Iskwewuk!
Wayahay, Wayaho! Wayahay, Wayahay, Wayaho!
Iskwewuk, niipawik! (Women, stand up)
Iskwewuk niipawik Iskwewuk!
Wayahay, Wayaho! Wayahay, Wayahay, Wayaho!
Iskwewuk bimoothdek! (Women, walk)
Iskwewuk, bimoothdek Iskwewuk
Wayahay, Wayaho! Wayahay, Wayahay, Wayaho!
Iskwewuk, nigamook! (Women, sing)
Iskwewuk, nigamook Iskwewuk
Wayahay, Wayaho! Wayahay, Wayahay, Wayaho!
Wayahay! Wayahay! Wayaho!
Wayahay! Wayahay! Wayaho!

This "Cree Woman's Song: Iskwewuk" calls upon women to take back their mind and body, to reclaim their whole self, so that they can stand up to violence around them and sing with power and pride! I sing this song for all Indigenous women who fight for a better life for themselves and their children.

—Brenda Wastasecoot, 2006

RESPONSE

As a nehiyaw iskwew (four-spirited woman), *Encounters at the 'Edge of Woods'* has been and will forever be one of the most powerful experiences of my life. I just happened to respond to an invitation that gifted me the opportunity to perform on stage and share my creative storytelling abilities. I simultaneously educated audiences about the appalling mistreatment of Indigenous Peoples in Canada with an emphasis on the experiences of Indigenous women. I am forever grateful to our courageous Anishinaabe Ashkenazi matriarch Jill Carter and my fellow story tellers within the Collective Encounter for allowing me to share my stories with them. When I reflect upon our story-weaving process, I find myself moved by how we shifted ourselves beyond the superficial, moving past our differences and allowing our stories to be placed alongside one another where they seemed to naturally honour the historic and present truths experienced by Indigenous Peoples, especially women. This was not purposefully designed, but I believe that the natural order of intention occurs when words are released from our mouths, ensuring spiritual alignment—words carry spirit and intention reveals itself. After all, we had gathered together to deeply consider the Indigenous experience in Canada and how we all wear it. We are all connected by the stories the land carries, and I felt the power of that connection as we listened to each other throughout the process of staging the play.

When we mounted the play in 2019, the #MeToo movement was at its height and women working within the entertainment industry were pushing back against its long history of sexual harassment and rape culture. I felt that our collective was joining the cause as it was comprised mostly of women, was led by a woman, and included the support of three young men. And we were mounting the first ever Indigenous play in the granddaddy of Canadian theatres, Hart House. Whether those three young men intended it or not, they were lifting up the voices of women and mirroring the nehiyaw matriarchal system that was practised before colonizing policies disempowered Indigenous women: "The woman was defined as nourisher, and the man, protector, and as protector, he had the role of helper. He only reacted: she acted. She was responsible for the establishment of all the norms—whether they were political, economic, social, or spiritual" (Royal Commission 17).

My fellow nehiyaw, Sylvia McAdam, writes about the authority of women in her book *Nationhood Interrupted: Revitalizing nehiyaw Legal Systems*:

> The women's teachings are the educational system of the *nêhiyaw* Nation. There existed a group of women called *okihcitâwiskwêwak* whose role was to provide the legal "system" of the *nêhiyaw* people . . . *nêhiyaw* women are the law keepers as well as knowledge keepers of the principles and customs of their people. [The meaning of *okihcitâwiskwêwak* is defined as clan mother or warrior woman] . . . During and prior to treaty making, it would have been the *okihcitâwiskwêwak* who would have been consulted regarding the land, because authority and jurisdiction to speak about land resides with the women . . . The power and authority of women was reflected in every aspect of the nation's activities. (24, 54, 55, 56)

NOKUM'S CALL

Nokum (my grandmother) Margaret Quinney could be described as one of the okihcitawiskwewak. Her Cree name was onaskwahamakes (the one who sings along). She was a medicine woman, a hunter, a trapper, a fisher, a fluent speaker of "high" or pure nehiyawewin (the Cree language), and a residential school survivor. She held the authentic knowledge of the signing of Treaty 6, knowledge passed on to her from her grandfather papakachas (Thin Stomach), also known as Simon Gadwa, who attended the signing at Fort Pitt in 1876. Through her lifetime, she testified in court on numerous occasions on behalf of the nehiyaw Nation, calling on the government to respect the land and treaty rights that had been agreed upon. In the 1960s, she became an elected councillor for her First Nation, Frog Lake, and was a founding member of its school (K–12). In July 1970, nokum and other parents organized a sit-in with the intention of taking over the Blue Quills (Sacred Heart) residential school. She ultimately led the physical takeover when she collected willows, entered the building, and whipped the nuns, physically removing them from the property. Her group demanded that then-Minister of Indian Affairs Jean Chrétien hand over control of the school to the community. After a prolonged battle, the parents prevailed, control of the school was turned over to the Native Education Council, and they transformed the buildings into Blue Quills College (nuhelot'įne thaiyots'į nistameyimâkanak), the first Indigenous-controlled educational institution in Canada. Today, it is the Blue Quills University. Nokum sat on the board for many years, supported by fellow warrior women Allison Makokis, Edith Memnoch, Theresa Gadwa, and many others. Nokum raised fourteen children, including my mother, nigawe (Jeanne Moyan) who, along with her younger siblings, survived the Blue Quills residential school. Nokum's lashing of the nuns could never match the intense physical, emotional, spiritual, and sexual abuse her children suffered at the hands of the Catholic nuns and priests who ran the school. But she tried.

Nigawe is pitihkohwatum (Rumbling Buffalo Woman), and she survived six years of unspeakable abuse at Blue Quills and witnessed the abuse of her siblings and many other children. She was taken to the school when nokum was out hunting to provide for the family. nomosom (my grandfather) wasn't around often, as he was in heavy recovery from his own residential school experience and from his service in WWII. My mother recalls the day her and her siblings were taken to the residential school. While they were at their grandparents' waiting for their mother to return, the RCMP pulled up and forcefully put the youngest ones in their police car. Several of the older ones ran into the forest and were terrorized by the police, who chased them down. My mother remembers trying to soothe the little ones to stop them from screaming and crying as they drove off. It took her some time to realize that she was screaming and crying along with them. It was like another voice far away inside her mind that she couldn't hear. She describes it like being put into prison, yet she was certain her mother would come for her. My grandmother never came, and it broke my mother's heart. They did not know that in 1920 the government had legally mandated the taking of Indigenous children to residential schools. It was illegal for nokum to retrieve her children.

RESPONSE TO NOKUM

"Onaskwahamakes"

the one that sings along

hear her scream in the woods?
as you sang your hunting song?

the one that sings along

she waited for you
punctured skin
braids gone

the one that sings along

protector?
protect her
provider?
provide her
healer?
heal her
its taken too long

the one that sings along

your whipping of nuns
did you soak the willow with their blood?
make them scream along?

the one that sings along

willow was the witness in your palm

nokum (my grandmother), onaskwahamakes (The One That Sings Along), a.k.a. Margaret Quinney. Photo courtesy of Trina Moyan.

CALL

You've had it! You're done! No more Mr. Nice Guy! No more bitches! (Collective Encounter)

RESPONSE

> *We were matriarchal and all those roles and responsibilities—everybody knew them. Now it's time to bring that knowledge base back to our students so they can feel confident and say, "Hey we don't have to buy into a hierarchy, we don't have to buy into a bureaucracy, we don't have to buy into patriarchy, we don't have to buy into competition because we are a collective."* (Dr. Leona Makokis, in Coyes)

My mother was SIXTEEN years old when she returned to Frog Lake, leaving the Blue Quills residential school with a grade SEVEN education, after spending six years there. Upon her return home, she had to begin day school, which was also run by Catholic nuns and priests. Ironically, the day school nuns ridiculed her for being older and so far behind in her grades. This was because she didn't do a lot of studying at the residential school, instead she was kept busy doing heavy labour for the nuns and priests to keep the school operational. She cleaned, cooked, washed, gardened, provided child care to the younger children. You name it, she did it—all while being abused. Her return home was painful as she mentally grappled with what she had experienced at Blue Quills. Now she was made to feel ashamed of herself at the day school, for being sixteen years old and the biggest kid in grade SEVEN. The nuns tortured her psychologically and the children bullied her, and throughout that she had to continue to carefully avoid the priests who sexually preyed on all of them. By the time she met my dad, who is Métis, that same year at the local general store, she was ready to escape it all and jumped at the opportunity to run away with him. They fell madly in love and stole away to Edmonton, Alberta, until their families called them back to get married; they were both only seventeen years old. They were excited to settle down and receive their land and house on Frog Lake, like all the other married couples, and begin their lives together. But immediately after the wedding, they were told that they had to leave Frog Lake because Mom was no longer considered an Indigenous woman. A sexist gender-based policy in the Indian Act saw Status men who married out (married non-Status women) keep their own Status and allowed their non-Indigenous wives to gain Status. The Indian Act is focussed on male land ownership.

Mom was excommunicated, stripped of her Status, and told that she gave it up because she had married a non-treaty Indian. notawe, my father, and his family were cheated out of their legal Indigenous identity by another assimilation policy, Métis Scrip, wherein families were offered pieces of land to farm. The land his family took was nearly unfarmable with little water to be found, and they were not told that accepting the land meant they were no longer legally considered "Indian." Neither of my parents knew anything about these policies defined in the 1876 Indian Act and how it would deeply impact their lives together.[1]

When the Indian Act was revised in 1951, it introduced even more discriminatory rules that disempowered Indigenous women. As a girl growing up and visiting Frog Lake every weekend, holiday, and for the length of the summer, I remember my parents talking at length about the white women who became Status Indians when they married Status men on our reserve. It was painful for my parents to witness these mixed-race couples raise their families in Frog Lake, especially as my parents were two Cree-speaking authentic nehiyaw people who were forced to raise their family off the reserve. Those couples received homes and land, but my parents struggled in poverty, fighting to make ends meet with limited education in the nearby racist town of Lloydminster. Cut off from their community, they felt abandoned, and it was another gouge at open psychological wounds inflicted by their childhood experiences. My mother was beyond hurt, and I saw her wince when standing next to white women living on the reserve who had Status. When I think of the current Missing and Murdered Indigenous Women, Girls, and Two-Spirit (MMIWG2S) movement and the Indigenous identity fraud that have become national crises, the connections are clear. The government intended to fracture

---

1 "The 1876 Indian Act also explicitly stipulated that any First Nations woman who married anyone other than an 'Indian' or 'non-treaty Indian' would themselves cease to be 'Indian' under the meaning of the Act" (Native Women's Association).

Indigenous identity through sexist policies that stripped First Nations women of their identities while allowing white women to get Status. Essentially, white women were given the legal underpinnings to play "red-face" while simultaneously humiliating and removing First Nations women from their traditional positions of authority. Métis lawyer Jean Teillet notes in her 2022 report about Indigenous identity fraud for the University of Saskatchewan, "Who are these fraudsters? Overwhelmingly they are settlers. In the academy, they are mostly women . . . Some of these fraudsters play heavily on Indigenous stereotypes of family violence, racism, and poverty" (12, 18). These fraudsters add insult to injury by creating convoluted lies to convince others that they experienced the violent history that Indigenous women like my mother and grandmothers and great grandmothers had actually survived. It is another assault on Indigenous women. Generations have been denied their identity as Indigenous women, including myself and my sisters, until 1985 when another group of warrior women raised their voices in protest.

CALL

No. It has gone on long enough. This is over.

This is over.
This is over.
This is over.
This is over.
This is over.
(Collective Encounter)

Four Indigenous women who had been stripped of their Status fought back. Mary Two-Axe Earley, Sandra Lovelace Nicholas, Yvonne Bédard, and Jeannette Corbiere Lavell led the way in changing the discriminatory sexist law. In 1985, the Indian Act was amended "by Bill C-31 to remove all sex-based distinctions affecting entitlement to register for status, but legal mechanisms to curtail the number of individuals entitled to Status remained, particularly through the second-generation cut-off rule" (Native Women's Association).

It was a bittersweet victory for Indigenous women who had been stripped of their Status and for their children who had been denied it. When my mother heard the news, she didn't believe it; when it finally sank in, she sat down and wept. I was THIRTEEN years old, and I held her hand as she cried, but she was not shedding tears of joy. She was releasing years of buried pain. I was witness to her pain, and I cried with her. She had hoped to move home and have her piece of land and a house near her siblings and parents, but she was placed at the bottom of the waiting list. At that point, lateral violence fed by the government's imposed elected Chief and Council system was rampant and she was not accepted back to Frog Lake Nation even with her reinstated Status. She and my father eventually bought a home from her younger brother so she could live on the reserve—she was in her late 50s. She poured herself into the land and grew a lifetime's worth of sweetgrass and became a respected community Elder. Her brothers made her the pipe she carries.

Bill C-31 excluded grandchildren. My two sons did not gain their Status until the law was amended in 2011 when Bill C-3 was passed, allowing Status to the grandchildren of women who had been reinstated in 1985. Yet those amendments continue to discriminate against Indigenous women and their descendants but not against Indigenous men. Again, this battle was led by an Indigenous warrior woman, Sharon McIvor, and is ongoing.

My parents survived but did not thrive for a long time, it took them most of their adult lives to recover from the assimilation policies that had injured them. Life was not easy growing up with the intergenerational trauma that shook the core of our family. But they did their best for me and my sisters, and we love them dearly for their enduring strength. They are beautiful souls, and we are blessed to still have them with us.

RESPONSE TO NIGAWE

"pitihkohwatum"

rumbling buffalo woman

they stripped you naked
forced you to roam
you faked painlessness

pounding your hooves in angry puddles of tears
running from it
sliding into the wet mess
peeled you off the ground
again and again and again
sometimes you were gone for weeks
slipping for years

hanging that glorious horned head down low
horns loosened by white women stealing your face

you finally offered your dried skull to the Sun Dance
neck sore from carrying it
thirsty days soaked in prayers healing you

now bellowing your sacred song
rumble on buffalo woman
rumble on

My mother in her regalia featuring the buffalo spirit she is named after, pitihkohwatum (Rumbling Buffalo Woman). Returning to ceremony helped my mother heal. She has passed her regalia, which was made by her mother, down to me. Photo courtesy of Trina Moyan.

CALL

They let go of my hands!
Where are my sisters?
Where are my sisters?
Where are my sisters?
Where are my sisters? Where are my sisters?
(Collective Encounter)

RESPONSE

Empowering women and girls empowers humanity.
(Jody Wilson Raybould 220)

I'm fifty years old and I just recently learned from my SEVENTY-SIX-year-old mother that she took my dried-up belly button and put it in a book because her prayer for me was to learn and have an education so I could survive in the white man's world. Clearly, I'm still not asking the right questions so I can receive these details about my own life.

Traditionally it was the okihcitawiskwewak, the midwives who served as sacred guides for new mothers; the okihcitawiskwewak welcomed newborns into the world with tradition of placing the belly button in the right location to ensure a good life path for the new being. My mom explained the tradition to me:

> The old wise women would take the belly button and pray that the lives of the children would be successful in connection to where that button was placed. I wanted you to be successful in life with an education. When your belly button fell off, right away I put it into a book. That's what I did. We didn't have a book shelf, but I always had stacks of books by my bed. My grandmother Isabelle Trottier Gadwa was a midwife and the other one [midwife] was Mrs. Dion, my cousin's mother. But before them there was a woman who was blind named notokwew Mary (old lady Mary). Everyone depended on her for births, and they would go pick her up [when she was needed]. She was

known by her touch and feel, and she was already very old when I remember her; when I saw her, I was a young girl. She was so old and so very intelligent; she spoke of many hard times, and she had so much experience. My mom always paid attention to the Elders, and this old lady would greet us with her hands on the top of our heads and she would feel with her fingertips all the way down to our feet. She did that to me and my brothers and all the new babies. It is the way it has always been with the nehiyaw people. When a child is first born, you take your baby to the oldest person in the family, and by placing your baby in their hands we are asking for blessings for that baby. It was the way I understood it—it was a blessing for the baby to grow up as an adult and become a good person.

My mother is the eldest in the family, and at my uncle's wake, she was passed the youngest of the family, Knoxley, to honour my uncle's life. Recognizing new life when one has passed on is the nehiyawak traditional way of giving thanks to Creator for the continuation of all life. Photo by Trina Moyan.

When I had my youngest son, Pearson, here in downtown Toronto, it was noon when she finally met him, so she faced apithakiskanohk (south, the half day) and thanked the Creator for her nosisim (grandson). She introduced herself to him in nehiyawewin:

> I asked the Creator to please bless this child's life. I thanked the Creator for you, my daughter, being alive because it was a hard birth. And I asked the Creator to bless him so he would be kind and smart. I faced the south because it was half the day when he was put into my arms. I asked the Creator to bless this little boy that was born to us—being loaned to us. I told him "I'm your kokum and I love you," and I kissed him. And then I began to think of his Cree name.

The women in my family, on both my mother's and father's sides, held immense medicinal and practical knowledge about keeping, making, and giving life. After my mother married my father, they moved to live with my father's family. My mother became very close to my chapan (great grandmother) Justine Moyan, who raised my father after his mother was forced to give him up when she was living with her abusive second partner. My mother shared her memories of my chapan with me:

> Your chapan, your little granny, delivered her own babies at home. There was twelve altogether. Six girls and six boys. All delivered at home except for one. She delivered her first baby all alone, her husband ran away because he was scared of her screaming. They were in a wagon, a covered wagon box. She said she suffered all by herself because her husband ran away. That's what she told us, and she was only seventeen. And so, it was no problem for her to deliver her babies on her own, and when her daughters started having babies, she was the midwife. She [chapan] miscarried a baby because her husband made her work hard, and wherever she walked, there was a trail of blood in the fresh snow. She couldn't stop the blood, and so she told her son Eddie who was twelve to go get help. He [Eddie] saw the little clump of blood in the snow, and when he went to the neighbours for help, he said his mother lost a kidney. Hahahaha.

> The other women came. Your chapan and those women were so smart, they knew which medicines to make to stop the bleeding. They knew all the medicines. Your chapan delivered so many babies in the community and [also] her own.

When listening to my mother share this story, I heard her laughter even though she acknowledged that my chapan was abused by her husband. My father speaks quietly of how he witnessed his grandmother being beaten by his grandfather. Chapan spoke to the Spirits, practiced strong medicine, and foretold the death of her husband. When she was ninety-nine-years-old and I was eleven, she lived with us; I sat with her every night, braiding her hair, and we laughed a lot. She lived to the age of 104. My chapan was powerful; and she told me to never get married. I didn't listen. I didn't understand why she would tell me that because I didn't know about the historical treatment of Indigenous women.

When the Europeans arrived with their patrilineal colonizing systems, they saw the power of Indigenous women and focused on destroying matrilineal governance.

> The role of Iroquois women in frontier diplomacy. Colonists who assumed that in Indian country as in the colonial world, men alone did public business carefully jotted down the names of all the native men attending the Lancaster Treaty (1744), but they did not list a single woman among the 100 or so who were there. Some observant Europeans knew that the women have a deliberative voice in their councils indeed that women were the soul of the councils . . . for while native men took the public stage to speak . . . native women stayed behind the scenes meeting in private to approve or disapprove proposals and agreements. (Merrell 28)

My chapan, Justine Moyan, with my mother and the future generations of our family. Photo courtesy of Trina Moyan.

CALL

Earth is Mother. And resource extraction equals violence on mother—equals rape—equals a breakdown of social relations—equals violence on other human bodies.
(Collective Encounter)

RESPONSE

> *So long as men have no respect for the land, they will have no respect for the women.* (Frances McAdam, qtd. in McAdam 40)

It is well documented that European men depended on Indigenous women during the 250-year fur trade economy. Indigenous women held extensive knowledge of the landscape, medicines, food, clothing, and matrilineal kinship connections that secured long-term allyship between European men and Indigenous Nations. Indigenous women were interpreters, negotiators; the Métis Nation was born from their interracial marriages to European men. Indigenous women were the backbone of the fur trade. Yet, they were largely discarded when European women began to arrive.

> By the mid-nineteenth century, settler society was developing a sharper sense of racial boundaries in marriage and association. HBC fur traders (especially the leading traders in the field) increasingly sought non-Indigenous wives. Indigenous women and women of mixed ancestry found themselves marginalized by social sanctions and by new settler-society legal codes that denied them a right to claim inheritances from their settler husbands. (Belshaw et al.)

CALL

Once I sat on an edge like this before.
(Collective Encounter)

Today's protests and demonstrations to protect waters and lands are led by Indigenous women, and disrespect toward women is reflected in the environmental damage taking place the world over. The history of disempowerment of Indigenous women on Turtle Island has left us vulnerable to violence and has touched almost all of the women in my family in some form.

In 2004, my cousin Rachel Quinney was murdered; it took two full years before her suspected killer was arrested. Turns out he was a serial murderer, and it took the police prioritizing the search for a missing white woman for Rachel's blood to be discovered on the killer's duffel bag. In September of 2021, my cousin Krystal Moyan's body was found at an intersection in Kelowna, British Columbia. The RCMP conducted a short investigation, but when my family inquired about whether the investigation was continuing, they received no official response. A month prior, in August 2021, Gabby Petito, a white girl, was murdered by her boyfriend, and her case was quickly solved and made international news. The amount of attention given to one white girl and the amounts of money spent on the investigation were in stark contrast to what my cousins received. In fact, a movie, *The Gabby Petito Story*, was released in 2022. Meanwhile, my family still has no answers about what happened to Krystal. The National Inquiry into Missing and Murdered Indigenous Women and Girls Final Report published the following statistics:

> In 2010, the Native Women's Association of Canada (NWAC) confirmed 582 cases over 20 years of missing or murdered Indigenous women and girls. In 2013, Maryanne Pearce, writing about missing and murdered women for her doctorate in law, identified 824 who were Indigenous. The mounting evidence spurred the Royal Canadian Mounted Police (RCMP) to do their own review, which confirmed 1,181 cases of "police-recorded incidents of Aboriginal female homicides and unresolved

> missing Aboriginal females" between 1980 and 2012. The RCMP report also stated that Indigenous women made up roughly 16% of all female homicides between 1980 and 2012, despite making up only 4% of the female population. Statistics, however, can be misleading: this number represents an average over a long time span, which obscures the increasing severity of the problem—namely, that Indigenous women and girls now make up 24% of female homicide victims. (National Inquiry)

Indigenous creation stories largely centre the female powers of creation for all of life on Mother Earth. Elder Wilfred Buck tells the Cree creation story of the Star People—achakos ininewuk ("N" dialect of Cree). The story beautifully depicts achakos iskwew (Star Woman) finding pakone kisik (The Hole in the Sky) through which she sees aski (Earth). Star Woman desires to visit aski and strikes a deal with kokominakasis (Grandmother Spider).

> achakos iskwew asked kokominakasis if she would send a single strand of webbing down through pakone kisik so she could come down to Earth to visit. kokominakasis told achakos iskwew she could but there were conditions she must accept. The first was that achakos iskwew must accept the condition that she would become a physical being when she entered this reality. achakos iskwew accepted. The next condition was that she could not return to the cosmos until after she gave up all she experienced while she visited Earth. Again, she accepted. Finally, kokominakasis said achakos iskwew had to bring a gift to this strange place so that all those to follow would be reminded of where it is they came from. achakos iskwew accepted. achakos iskwew came to this place to experience, learn, teach, and explore. Through her we all come to this place through that single strand of webbing—the umbilical cord—to also visit, experience, learn, teach, and explore. We accept a physical form, and when we leave, we give up all that has become dear to us. The gift that was left for us by achakos iskwew is achakos ahtakoop (the star blanket). We are Star Children. (Pawaminikitititicikiw 28)

Rachel and Krystal have made their journey home back to the stars as descendants of the okihcitawiskwewak (warrior women) along with the many other Indigenous women, girls, and Two-Spirit folk who have been taken too soon.

RESPONSE TO RACHEL AND KRYSTAL

"achakos nisimis"

Star Sister

palm wet with blood from a clenching grip

hanging desperate to spider's downy edge

sway with mouth wide open to witness the weaving of relatives

face bones shimmering with remains of their makings

brow etched by golden headdress

moist luminous thread to the gentle release

humming hover as benevolent feet immerse in golden earth

hearts gaze and gasp giving thanks

grandfather Sun fades in your brilliance

stay Star Sister

ekosi maka (enough for now)

My painting of achakos iskwew on my gardening jacket. A self-reminder to take pride in the matrilineal lineage that I am born of when I plant medicines. Photo by Trina Moyan.

Anishinaabe Ashkenazi matriarch Jill Carter is gifted a star blanket. She wove our stories together, creating *Encounters at the 'Edge of the Woods.'* It is a reminder to celebrate our warrior women who often stand at the edge of the world fighting for our collective health and to keep our promise to kokominakasis (Grandmother Spider) to never forget where we come from. Photo by Connor Pion.

WORKS CITED

Belshaw, John, with Sarah Nickel and Chelsea Horton. *Histories of Indigenous Peoples and Canada*. Thompson Rivers University. https://histindigenouspeoples.pressbooks.tru.ca/front-matter/acknowledgement/.

Coyes, Gregory, dir. *Blue Quills Acimowin*. Bearpaw Media Productions, 1 January 2005.

McAdam, Sylvia. *Nationhood Interrupted: Revitalizing nehiyaw Legal Systems*. Vancouver: Purich Publishing, 2016.

Merrell, James H., ed. *The Lancaster Treaty of 1744: With Related Documents*. New York: Bedford/St. Martin's, 2008.

National Inquiry into Missing and Murdered Indigenous Women and Girls. *Reclaiming Power and Place: The Final Report of the National Inquiry into Missing and Murdered Indigenous Women and Girls*. Volume 1A. https://www.mmiwg-ffada.ca/final-report/.

Native Women's Association of Canada. "Indian Act." 2023. https://nwac.ca/policy/indian-act.

Pawaminikititicikiw [Wilfred Buck]. *Kitcikisik (Great Sky) Tellings That fill the Night*. Six Nations of the Grand River Territory: Indigenous Education Press, 2021.

Royal Commission on Aboriginal Peoples. "Women's Perspectives." In *Perspectives and Realities*. Vol. 4 of *The Final Report of the Royal Commission on Aboriginal Peoples*. 1996. https://www.bac-lac.gc.ca/eng/discover/aboriginal-heritage/royal-commission-aboriginal-peoples/Pages/final-report.aspx.

Teillet, Jean. *Indigenous Identity Fraud: A Report for the University of Saskatchewan.* 17 October 2022. https://leadership.usask.ca/documents/about/reporting/jean-teillet-report.pdf.

Wilson-Raybould, Jody. *From Where I Stand: Rebuilding Indigenous Nations for a Stronger Canada.* Vancouver: Purich, Books, 2019.

Second Thoughts: A Postmortem at the Edge of the Woods

GRACE PHAN-NGUYEN AND JENNIFER ALICIA MURRIN

INTRODUCTION

On June 3, 2022, Grace Phan-Nguyen, who was in Berlin, Germany, and Jennifer Alicia Murrin, who was in Toronto, Canada, met via Zoom to have the following conversation. Based on their experiences as cast members in *Encounters at the 'Edge of the Woods,'* this conversation is about the process of creating the play. This conversation was also informed by other Indigenous and non-Indigenous participants' experiences, which were gathered through an anonymous Google survey and interviews via Zoom. The names of these participants have been left out for privacy purposes.

Grace and Jennifer agree that the process and creation of this play had an immense impact on them as individuals and that this was the first time they had been part of a project like this.

GRACE: Hey Jennifer, thanks so much for jumping into this conversation with me! We both know each other but would you like to introduce yourself again for this conversation?

JENNIFER: Sure. So, my name is Jennifer Alicia Murrin. I am Mi'kmaq and also settler, with German, Irish, and Scottish ancestry. I'm originally from Elmastukwek, Ktaqmkuk (Bay of Islands, Newfoundland), but I currently live in Toronto. I was part of the Indigenous cast for *Encounters.*

GRACE: My name is Grace Phan-Nguyen. I am part of the non-Indigenous counterpart for the *Encounters* ensemble. I am of Vietnamese descent, and I was born and raised in Tkaron:to.

We're here today to talk about our experiences with this process of going through irreconcilable spaces as a creation development, but also to share some of the voices that graciously gave input about their own experiences.

We've interviewed individuals from the Indigenous and non-Indigenous people who were part of the play. And we've compiled this discussion around these questions: How did you feel at the beginning, during and after this process? What went well? What didn't go well? We hope that this chapter will help those who are interested in this practice of reflection for their own projects to look at their motivations and to take into account ways to adapt to co-creators' needs.

Jenn, would you be so kind to talk about the principles used in *Encounters*? To be fair, this is more than two years after we've done this performance and created this work.

JENNIFER: So, my understanding is that Jill brought in this idea of irreconcilable spaces to the cast. She got it from Métis curator David Garneau, who talks about the "irreconcilable spaces of Aboriginality." He says that reconciliation is not achievable because at one point there had to have been some sort of respectful relationship, and he argues that settlers never gave Indigenous Peoples such respect. But he does say that conciliable spaces are achievable, but there needs to be this time of an irreconcilable space. And so, with *Encounters at The Edge Of The Woods*, what we created were those irreconcilable spaces. Throughout the process, we worked through those spaces to navigate and figure out if we were able to achieve conciliation at the end of this process and this play. Part of it is standing at the edge of the woods where this irreconcilable space is taking place—encounters at the edge of the woods. Ultimately, to look at whether or not we've reached the edge of the woods, if we've come together at the edge of the woods, if we're still standing at the edge of the woods, or if we've been welcomed or we've welcomed folks into the woods. And so that was the general idea of it all.

GRACE: Thanks, Jenn! During this process, the non-Indigenous participants had the ability to also have our own separate groups for white settler participants and the BIPOC participants. And this was happening simultaneously with the Indigenous counterparts working in their own spaces. The moments of conciliation, or the facilitated time of creating together, were normally where we would bring what we had from our respective workshops and then try to find a through line or common thread to tie it all together.

And Jill Carter, our director, was the person who guided all of us through this process. She invited witnesses to observe and document what was happening in the space. She took our reflections, collaborations, and written work to make a mosaic of a final performance. Jill really had a gift of finding these pieces that related to each other and then finding the story. We ended up having this two-hour long play that essentially put everyone's work into it. She only cut things out when it was absolutely necessary. And so, it was like a behemoth of a script that you can read in this book.

Some of the questions we have asked were created specifically for Indigenous and non-Indigenous folks—essentially, what we were trying to get at was, what are your thoughts and feelings about the methodology for creating this play? And were there moments that felt uncomfortable—or what was that dynamic of being in an Indigenous-only space and then being with non-Indigenous folks afterwards (or vice versa)? I think when you were asked to join this process, Jenn, as a settler/Indigenous person, did you feel like you had to approach the edge of the woods and have that responsibility of inviting the non-Indigenous folks?

JENNIFER: I think when I signed up for this, I didn't have any idea what I was getting myself into. I think that, like a lot of the folks who ended up being part of this project, there were two things. There was the actual play, like the product, and then there was the process. And for me as a mixed person, in the beginning, it was awkward because I'm like, where do I sit as someone who has both settler and Indigenous ancestry? I ended up sitting with the Indigenous cast. But I did have moments of awkwardness because when I was addressing the settlers for me as an individual, as a person, I also recognized that some of my ancestors were standing on the other side of the edge. My maternal grandmother is German and Scottish. I also have Irish ancestry on my maternal and paternal side. Those families came here to Canada and settled on stolen land. This is my family history and therefore, part of my story, too. And so, there were those moments of awkwardness and unsettled feelings. I didn't express this to the group. I went along with the process, and perhaps this was something I should have addressed.

GRACE: When I was asked to join this process, I definitely felt a heavy responsibility. I felt like I had to creatively contribute as much as I could without the expectation that all of it was going to be used in the final script, as we were centring Indigenous voices. It was a tension and pressure that I haven't experienced in a Westernized theatre creation process. Actually, some of our non-Indigenous folks who did answer our survey responded to the question, "If you're not Indigenous, how did you approach the edge of the woods when working with Indigenous cast members?" And a lot of people mentioned that they were listening a lot instead of speaking—specifically to the stories that the Indigenous participants shared. And then some people felt a responsibility to incorporate their own story and experiences in reaction to hearing those stories, and they had to be mindful of not overstepping. Trying to navigate that for themselves was quite challenging.

And it was very interesting because being creative also demands taking that space and bringing our sense of selves forward because we're all complex individuals that want to be heard. I also remember one of our Indigenous cast members, when we interviewed them, they mentioned that even in the Indigenous cast there were so many nuances and experiences that were not collectively shared that definitely put some tension in the process as well, which is parallel to the non-Indigenous cast members.

JENNIFER: I remember in one of our conversations with an Indigenous cast member, one of the things that they brought forward was around welcoming non-Indigenous cast members to the edge of the woods. They asked, "Do I have the right to do the welcoming?" And then went on to say non-Indigenous folks have to want to be invited before we, the Indigenous cast, does the welcoming. Navigating those moments was quite awkward at times during the creative process because we literally had exercises where we stood facing one other. And even that in itself kind of felt like we were standing at the edge of the woods.

GRACE: There's also the fear of messing up or doing something wrong and then ruining the process. During the development of the play, it was really interesting for me to witness the result of Jill's discernment and finding willing participants. I'm assuming that she decided whether they were informed or were aware enough of the history experienced by the Indigenous counterparts. Additionally, she would have had to evaluate if they were open to participating in these irreconcilable spaces where they'd be forced to face their biases while trying to not take up space when working with the Indigenous participants. I can't imagine the fine balance act Jill had to perform to make sure that the facilitation of irreconcilable spaces would allow our Indigenous participants to feel protected and safe enough to practise and tell their stories around non-Indigenous participants. So there's a screening process that I think happened way before this entire process of developing and staging the play. And during the actual execution of the play's development, we were wrestling with ourselves and this environment to bring forth the work, the art, and the history that we were trying to find commonality in.

JENNIFER: You mentioned willing participants, and I agree: you have to want to be invited. I think that is one thing we did achieve. I think everyone that was there wanted to be there and really cared about what we were doing. So that's step one. But then we have to work through the irreconcilable spaces and weave our stories together.

GRACE: Yeah—in the irreconcilable spaces and having to work through that. It caused me as a non-Indigenous cast member to really look at how much space I was taking up and made me reflect on some of the biases I've had. If I wasn't willing, this self-reflection work would not have happened.

It also put me in a place where I was very insecure about contributing and trying to find that balance of participating enough and participating too much. I had to negotiate with myself. How much is too much of my story? And should I always be proactively asking for input from the Indigenous cast? Which is also putting me in a cycle of, like, am I asking too much labour from our Indigenous counterparts?

Which leads us to one of the questions we posed at the beginning of the interview process about the development process: "What are your thoughts and feelings about the methodology used during the creative process?" Indigenous and non-Indigenous cast members mentioned that this was a necessary space for the Indigenous participants. I was wondering if you wanted to talk about how they felt going through this development process.

JENNIFER: We heard from an Indigenous cast member that they felt the group was very kind. The cast that Jill invited to be part of this project all really seemed to want to be there and wanted to be part of this and saw it as important. One of the most profound moments that stood out for this cast member was when Brenda told her story about watching her siblings get taken away. The cast member was watching the non-Indigenous cast members listening and witnessing Brenda's story. This was a profound moment. But then the questions came up: "Okay, I've listened to the story. I've witnessed the story. I'm aware of this. But what's next? What else can we do? Where do we go from here?" They also mentioned that maybe this is all beautiful and wonderful that we were witnessing these stories, but maybe we were not actually in the woods yet. Maybe we were still at the edge, maybe we were still processing, maybe we were still reflecting, and maybe we were not actually at a place where we could be in the woods together. So that was something that someone from the Indigenous cast mentioned. I don't know if you wanted to share any thoughts from the non-Indigenous side.

GRACE: Yes. I mentioned before that the non-Indigenous cast members also agreed that it was necessary to make this type of space because stories like Brenda's sometimes needed to be witnessed by the Indigenous cast members first. Then the stories can be shared in the spaces where non-Indigenous cast members were present.

There were some profound moments that a non-Indigenous interviewee shared where they felt like they were included and made to feel like they were part of a family. And it was clicking for them as to how they could support others creatively. However, they also had moments where they felt, artistically, a division even when the process was demanding some co-creation. So they felt a little bit excluded and at other times felt like they were included. Which is a really interesting note to take.

JENNIFER: And I think that's part of what I'm wondering—if that's just part of this process. The fact that, like you mentioned earlier, we were split into groups. We have moments where just the Indigenous cast met and just the non-Indigenous cast met. And then, even with the non-Indigenous cast, there were separate meetings as well, depending on your intersectional identities. And so I felt that created some divisions in a way because I started to look at non-Indigenous cast members in a certain way. But maybe that was the point.

GRACE: Yeah. I think the separation was needed because not everyone had a chance to talk about their experiences, whether it's traumatic or moments of joy. It doesn't need to be a sad story fest, right? But it's also sharing jokes and feeling safe to express yourself in either cultural or language specificity that isn't shared by other folks without that fear of judgment. I also think it helps to have a sounding board that reflects what you're saying. It gives you that confidence to share in a way that you feel empowered when you're sharing your stories to people outside of your community.

So I think the process has a lot of pros and cons. And depending on the end goal of what the project wanted to create, it served its purpose for sure. What this practice of irreconcilable spaces doesn't lend itself to is allowing people's complex identities to be fully explored because of either financial, time, facility, and/or resource limitations. One of the non-Indigenous persons of colour really struggled with being put into the settler's counterpart or being labelled "settler" because they didn't subscribe themselves to this term and what it entailed—referring to their ancestors and their unique history that did not fit the mould.

They essentially said that they mentally checked out and they were just there to contribute creatively. But they didn't know how to be the emotional support or to bring more togetherness or unity into their practice because they felt like they were being punished for the wrongdoings of white ancestors that they had no connection to. And I'm wondering, in retrospect, if it would have been beneficial for us to sit down to not only talk about the methodology and the practice, but to also put in guidance or guidelines for people to navigate the space in those moments. Like, should we have had more non-Indigenous, non-white spaces for us to wrestle with the fact that we're all living on Turtle Island and about how we got there? And is there a space for that?

JENNIFER: Right. The stories we were trying to tell in the play were also part of the process. It felt like an experiment in a way. We were all joined together. Not everyone knew everybody, but some of us knew each other. I knew some of the Indigenous cast. And we were all just brought together, a big group of us. And we were trying to work through this as we went along. We were trying to learn about each other. I feel like we just hit the ground running.

GRACE: Are you saying that we were not only creating work, but we were simultaneously exploring or experimenting with a whole new practice that we had no context of beforehand? We were trying to figure out each other, this process, and also creating art.

JENNIFER: Yeah. And getting to know people can be challenging, and we had such a big group, and the tensions were already there.

GRACE: Yeah, definitely. I can't imagine the tension for the Indigenous side because I wasn't in the spaces held for them. But I know that one of our non-Indigenous cast members did share with us that their work was not settler-like. So trying to find space for it felt really challenging for them. And the net that caught that story and brought it into the foreground was definitely Jill's supervision because she identified it and said, "Yes, let's go with it" and then, "What are the other stories that are related to this story?"

I think for the purpose of creation, I would have liked to have more time to get to know other participants better because during the process we were focused on creating theatre. But we were not focused on the individual relationship building or we didn't have the time to get to know each other to say, "Hey, I remember in a conversation you told me that you were really into planting, and you have a cat." And I'm wondering if we can bring that sort of playfulness into the creation process.

For example, one of the things that was really interesting to witness was how the Indigenous participants threw in a lot of dark humor in reaction to some of the stories because that's how they cope with the things that have happened to them historically. But I don't feel like I have the authority to talk about that.

JENNIFER: Yeah, I think humor is definitely healing, and it's definitely an important aspect for Indigenous folks, for sure. And I think some of the ways that we were able to incorporate that into this play and in this process was with one of Jenny's characters, Candy Girl, who started the show by walking through the crowd and just yelling at people to put their phones away and telling them the show is about to start. I think that's part of that humor. Also, the displays that we had in the lobby and the entrance to the theatre where there were boxes of water, and they were Justin Trudeau's tears: it referred to the signs above the water fountain in Hart House that talked about the fact that so many First Nations don't have access to clean drinking water.[1] I think this is where we were able to bring in that dark humor. I wasn't in the lobby, but it would be interesting to witness audience members when they entered that space just to see their reactions to all of that. So yeah, I think those were some of the ways that we were able to bring humor into this project, which I think was extremely important.

And I think, on your note about having a space to get to know each other, for me personally, it already takes me a while to get to know people just because of trauma. It takes a while for me to get comfortable with folks. And so that added another layer to it. I came in as a person who's already hesitant to meet new people, to be comfortable and open with new people, and then on top of that, we were then broken into Indigenous and non-Indigenous groups. That added some tension for me, and I didn't realize it at the time. But further along in the process, I recognized that is actually what was happening in terms of the way that I was interacting with people. So the process was actually influencing the way that I just talked to the artists, the cast, regular folks who were part of this project. So that was interesting. The process definitely influenced the way that I interacted with other cast members, but I'm not sure if this was the case for others, I'm just speaking for myself. I know that there were moments of tension that I've heard from the Indigenous cast members.

GRACE: Yeah, for sure. Actually, maybe we should talk about the installation for a bit because this creation process was not limited to theatre work, but it also lent itself to sound design, visual art, and set design. I think that's also a really great strength of this development practice because witnesses would come in—witnesses are people who are invited into the space to hear the stories and be inspired to create something from the stories that they've heard. And I think that's also a really great way

1 See "Pre-Show Installation" on page 105.

of protecting yourself and your story by inviting the people you know who will take it seriously. And then their reflection on the story that you shared is also very important. Can I read some responses from the non-Indigenous artists about what is the most important teaching they received while being part of this production?

JENNIFER: Yeah, sure.

GRACE: So, I have four responses that I think summarize some of the takeaways that non-Indigenous folks have. The first one says, "There are more stories hidden from people who do not have the space to narrate their stories and experiences." Another person responded with, "It is more impactful to listen rather than speak." Another teaching someone learned is "how to apply Dish with One Spoon [teachings] to my everyday life, how to tighten my belt to ensure that everyone has enough." And the last one is "the importance of collaboration and the freedom to create. It was an enriching experience to write alongside so many talented artists."

What do you think this process achieved? We have a play, so that's something that it achieved. I think it's important work that we did, and also the final product really spoke to the endurance that we have as a cast because the rehearsal process was incredibly demanding, not only physically and mentally, but emotionally. It required to you to be there at 110 per cent.

JENNIFER: Yeah, I agree. The process was challenging because not only were we creating together, we were collaborating together, we were trying to story-weave. Like, finding those threads in between our individual stories that we can pull together and create a scene or a piece in the play. Not only were we creating as artists, but then, like you said, there's all the other things—it's those irreconcilable spaces, there's those tensions that we were dealing with, there's getting to know people. So the process was definitely challenging, but I think we did something special with this play, for sure. This is the first time I've ever been—I mean, I'm also not experienced—but this was the first time I've ever been part of something like this. And it was very intense. We had late nights, and I would go home at night and find it hard to go to sleep because I was still reflecting on what we did earlier in our meeting and our sessions. But we got a play out of it. The first Indigenous play at Hart House in 100 years, which is exciting! And I got to meet lots of cool people like yourself!

GRACE: Aww, thanks! Takes one to know one. I think another thing that this practice definitely achieved was putting the non-Indigenous folks in a very reflective mindset, not only on their positioning, but also the stories that they were witnessing—Indigenous and non-Indigenous. There was and is a lot of hurt that exists on both sides, but there's very different ways of addressing it. And you can definitely see it in the script, in the storytelling, how people cope with their artwork or their art-making. And this theatre piece really shows the diversity of skills and practice within our ensemble.

JENNIFER: Yeah. It's interesting because not only are we artists, but now we were also kind of—I would say—forced to be part of this. Let me back up. So, we were all part of this play as artists, so we came in as actors, performers, whatever to be part of this play. Not only are we artists, but we were also thrown into this process where we were looking at ourselves as individuals, us as people. And it was interesting to try to balance where the line stops: Is there a line where it stops where I'm, like, an artist or where I'm just Jennifer Alicia? Or am I just me, Jennifer Alicia, in this play because we all brought in our own personal stories as well? So, it was hard to differentiate at times, too. And I can't imagine the pressure or responsibility folks might feel for being part of something like this as an individual and as an artist. Sarah Michaels's apology at the end of the play—I don't know how Sarah felt about that, but that was such a big moment. So, is it Sarah saying the apology, or is it Sarah the artist saying the apology, or is it both?

GRACE: Yeah, for sure. I also think that this creation process and being invited to this project made me really excited because it allowed me to witness Indigenous and non-Indigenous artists' practices in person. Because before the play's development, we talked about equity and diversity and the history the university is built upon and the land that it took from Indigenous communities in classes, but we were never challenged to take these teachings into practice.

Now I use various terms like, "I'm holding my own bundle to move forward." And I have learned from Lee Maracle who came in with her daughter Columpa Bobb to teach us about not only the story of the double-headed snake, but how to take agency to retell the Creation story and not have the pressure of it being exact. Because there's supposed to be variation, it's supposed to be alive and it's supposed to be moving forward, like, evolving. The core elements are still there, but the story itself is expected to change. And I think that was so eye-opening to the process because it was asking us to retell our own stories in a way that pushed us to not be trapped in our personal stories. There was a lot of stories of trauma and for us to reimagine it in a way that not only was safe for us, but was also easily shareable to our cast members.

And I think the intention of the process was not necessarily to invite us into the woods, but to make us all want to be at the edge of the woods to have that conversation. I think this process left us all asking, "Have we reconciled?" I think if we were to do this again and refine the development process, we have to admit that there are limitations to this process as well, because no process is perfect for each individual with all these intersectional identities. But something that could make this process a bit more manageable is having a smaller cast and setting expectations around inner conflict, contribution, and communication.

In the face of practices that you're unfamiliar with, ask yourself if these expectations are constructive or whether they are just going to divide the cast more. I find that type of negotiation is really important. And at the end of this development process and with the final product, I feel very proud to have created the work because it is important, and it's one of the most impactful rehearsal processes or creation processes that I've been a part of in my career in theatre and as an artist. This practice centring irreconcilable spaces brought so much creative and personal value to the play's development. I really think I would like to see it be practiced more. Maybe in our remount we could refine the work and see the story evolve in a way that honours the spirit of the Indigenous storytelling principles.

JENNIFER: Yeah, I agree with maybe a smaller cast. One thing I appreciate about Jill bringing everyone together is that she has the most interesting network of people. There were students, staff, and professors from the University of Toronto (U of T) and then folks that Jill knew from the theatre world outside of U of T and other spaces as well. And that's lovely. The cast was definitely, I think, a great representation of folks that we needed to be part of the story. I think that's why it was a two-hour play. But I do appreciate trying to include everyone in this work. And I think this process was heavy and it was hard and beautiful and all of these things. But we didn't have a chance for various reasons to have a debrief after. And I feel like I've been able to debrief a little bit, you know, working with you, Grace, on this project together and then interviewing other cast members for this as well.

So, I feel like I've had a bit of a debrief in taking on this chapter, but it was kind of like, "We did the play and then that was it." I've also heard from a few other folks that it would have been helpful to have a conversation after to talk about a lot of things that we've actually tried to address with this chapter. For example, the feedback and self-reflection about this process and the play. If it was done after the play finished, that would have been helpful. I didn't have an opportunity to necessarily chat with everyone every time we had a working session or practice. It's long hours, it's tiring, it's intense. I don't necessarily want to talk to people after our meetings. So, I was wondering how a lot of folks felt, like, even in our conversations, you've shared about things that have happened when the non-Indigenous participants met separately, and the Indigenous group maybe is unaware of what's going on over there. So, I found myself often thinking about other people's thoughts about this whole thing.

GRACE: I totally agree. So, hopefully, we can bring a "post-mortem" on paper here for our cast members. In conclusion, reflecting on the play's development and staging: one, it's really great. It really lends itself to the community aspect of creation. It allows us to make sure all voices are heard and creating spaces that allow BIPOC people to voice their journey and their stories. It allows participants to celebrate each other. And it also allows historically oppressed counterparts to share with their historically oppressing counterparts—when they position themselves as listeners and witnesses. I think this creative practice requires more points of contact where everyone has a chance to (a) get to know each other more and definitely have a post-mortem where people can talk about what they were wrestling with during the creation process, things to celebrate together, but also to walk with each other when we are wrestling with something that we didn't find an answer for during our work and (b) having a smaller cast would allow all this to happen more freely. This puts the onus on whoever is guiding the process, either the director or whoever is facilitating this creative development, to not only screen the people that would come into these very vulnerable spaces, but also to balance the needs of the participants that they are collaborating with.

So, it's not only inviting individuals who are from various walks of life into this creative process, but also knowing that they're going to be open enough provide and receive constructive critique.

I wanted to also thank you personally for taking the time to not only be part of the production, but also during this writing process. I learned a lot from you and am learning how to be a better friend. I'm very thankful for the relationships that came out of this process. And I'm very grateful as well for the patience that has been extended to me.

JENNIFER: Thanks for continuing to talk to me. When we had our practices and meetings, I think we were often there before everyone. We would be the folks—part of the group—who were there before the call time. And then you would just talk to me. And I'd be like, "Why is this person talking to me?" I was like, "Oh, okay, they're cool." I'm grateful that you continue to push—but not in an aggressive way—and talk to me and that we were able to form this friendship. And thank you for continuing to push me throughout this process, prompting me and reminding me. Just your willingness and your desire to get this done in a good way really helped me move forward with this. So, I definitely appreciate you for doing that and for asking to do this together.

CONCLUDING THOUGHTS

We thank Jill Carter for her guidance during this production and during this writing period. Her wisdom and gentle fighting spirit sustained us as we toiled and wrestled with our beings.

As we conclude this chapter, many things have come to light as of 2022. Since 2019, unmarked graves of Indigenous children have been discovered, National Reconciliation Day has been instituted in Canada, Pope Francis apologized to Indigenous Peoples in Canada, and it has become more noticeable that people protest on Canada Day by wearing orange to acknowledge the fraught history of this nation. We sense a shift in society and our pessimistic selves are cautious of it. Indigenous Peoples have been telling their stories for years and have been continuously silenced. It was not until Canada was faced with undeniable proof that the shift began.

To continue this momentum, we encourage you, the reader, to take the principles of *Encounters at the 'Edge of the Woods'* to your own artistic practice and everyday life. As you can see from our conversation, it doesn't have to be perfect, but it puts you in a place where you can learn to listen in preparation to be invited into the woods.

Canada is forced to face the edge of the woods. And it's time that Canada chooses to listen.

Lee

SHEILAH MADONNA MORTEL SALVADOR

Lee Maracle Calls out in Story from the 'Edge of the Woods.'
Production video and still by Tash Naveau.

I'll never forget the time I ran into Lee in the kitchen of First Nations House at the University of Toronto, once upon a time, before COVID. She looked me straight in the eye and said, "Hello, Sheilah." I was elated, flattered that she knew me—that she remembered my name! I must be one of the shiniest of stars amongst the countless students she encountered on a daily basis! Then I realized that I was still wearing my name tag from the workshop I attended a few hours ago. I had to laugh as I sat down to eat my lunch. Typical Lee, sassy and mischievous even in the softest, most quiet ways.

I took all the classes I could with her, went to all the events she was at, just so I could be in the periphery of her indomitable force and energy. I wanted to absorb what I could so I could become the strong and talented writer that I hope to be. I learned so much from her stories and teachings that I never got tired of hearing them over and over again and in different ways. I'll always admire her patience and kindness, which I did not expect from an icon. She always let people speak, and she listened, *really* listened, teaching us all to do the same so that we could navigate this world in the most authentic and loving way.

She did make me cry once, when in front of class she told me that my writing was poetic. At the time, I was really struggling with my path and with my confidence in myself, in my skills. At that moment, Lee told me what I needed and wanted to hear.

Right before the pandemic, she told me that she would invite me over when she had one of her poetry sessions with her friends on the porch of her house, which, I knew from her stories, to be solar-powered and flanked by sage, tobacco, and the three sisters: corn, beans, and squash.

I never got to go, but that invitation will always be a reminder of how she made me feel like a star who was about to "take flight." That is the wonder and miracle of Lee, always sharing her light and lifting others up, and I, along with the countless people she has touched and inspired, will always be grateful.

Maraming salamat, Lee, sa susunod na lang, until we meet again.

Bringing Spirit to the Telling

TASH NAVEAU

Lee Maracle Calls out in Story from the 'Edge of the Woods.'
Production video and still by Tash Naveau.

Upon first recording the story of the Double-Headed Serpent with Lee Maracle, the projectionist Nicole Eunju Bell, and myself present, the story seemed to feel like a lucid dream to me. The kind where you wake up and you know something important was just transmitted to you and you'd better remember it. What was also impressed upon me was that Lee spoke of how the story, in her Stó:lō teachings, was never supposed to be the exact same with each telling. The storyteller is expected to bring their own persona and spirit to the telling and what parts are told or possibly left out depends on who the audience is, who is listening. Prophecies are often warnings or cautionary stories that are told from experience, wisdom, and the beyond—our ancestors wanting better for us.

The final videos, layered and then mapped by Nicole for the projections in the play, came about in quite an organic way. I was given much freedom to explore what they might look like for this story and knew that I had to involve water. I had taken a video, using my cellphone, of the mountains and water when I was in Squamish territory the summer before. This seemed fitting for the background, along with blowing cedar bows that framed and almost enveloped Lee as she told the story. For the side panels, I used video recorded while on a canoe trip that I took with Nicole and Andrew Kesik, one day to Toronto Island, another significant site of Indigenous place-keeping and gathering—of peoples and for gathering of medicines. The video, depicting us paddling along the inner channels of the island, was later layered and flipped so that the two sides panels showed two canoes travelling next to each other, peacefully.

Two Canoes. Production video and still by Tash Naveau.

Encounters at the 'Edge of the Woods' Pre-Show Installation

JENNY BLACKBIRD

At the entrance to the theatre, the text of the 1884 Amendment to the Indian Act (the Potlatch Ban) reminds audiences of the suppression of Indigenous ceremonial observance and performative expression (dance, prayer, song, regalia) across this nation. Meanwhile, John Lennon's "Imagine" is played at half-tempo and punctuated by the sound of railway spikes being driven into the ground. The Potlatch Ban continued in Canada until 1951.

STOLEN LAND

I originally created this image years ago and posted it on Twitter as a response to someone else's decolonial meme. I'm not very popular on Twitter, so it didn't get much traction. So, I was glad that I was able to share this digital meme with the production and I hope that it really made people think about how Indigenous lands in "Canada" continue to be stolen from Indigenous Peoples.

CANDY GIRL STAND

The Candy Girl Stand was fun to make. Originally, I didn't plan on being in the production or on stage—I just wanted to contribute some visual art to the project. I thought about the food that Indigenous Peoples would eat pre-contact: from the land, foraged, hunted, planted/harvested, or fished from various waters. The food post-contact, and especially in the twentieth and twenty-first centuries, is not as good as what our ancestors ate back before assimilation really took hold. I decided that instead of a being a cigarette girl with a cigarette tray, I could be the candy girl. I was envisioning having candy in my tray, or even fake treaties. During our workshopping discussions, we spoke about having fake treaties to hand out to every audience member to sign.

I proposed setting up the Candy Girl Stand in the lobby. On one side, I hand painted the five "white gifts": flour, sugar, salt, milk, and lard—all the ration foods the government gave our ancestors. They are foods that aren't so great for anybody but foods that really affect Indigenous Peoples's health in awful ways. On the other side I painted wild game meat, fish, berries, corn, beans, squash, wild rice. All the good, nutritious foods that our ancestors ate. Those are the foods that we still do eat, and they are so much better for our health. Unfortunately, as we know, it is getting increasingly hard to get fresh fish and game meat or to find safe spots to forage, plant, and harvest. I even made a pamphlet that was very tongue-in-cheek, because Candy Girl is very clownish, and she was asking you whether you would prefer to eat the five white gifts, which might cause you harm, or would you rather eat the good foods from the land and from the waters that are not GMO.

TRUD'EAU

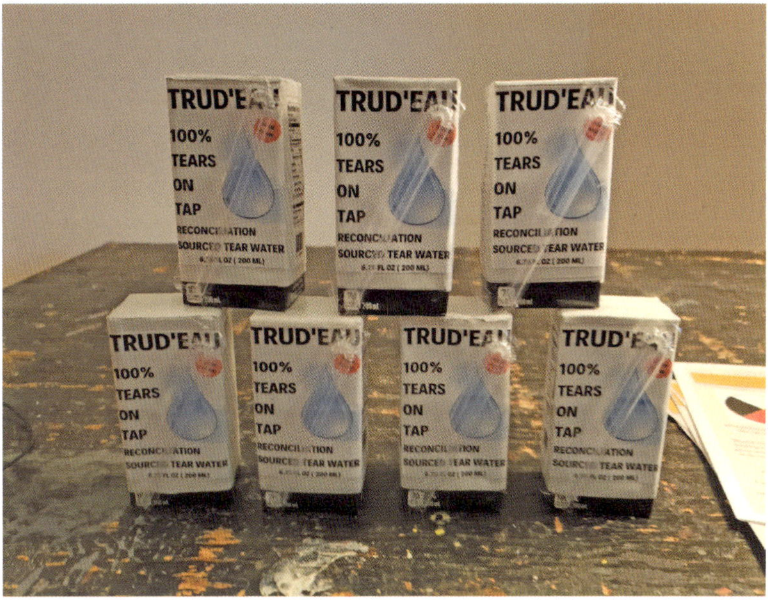

The Trud'eau boxed water labels were fun to make—a play on his name and the French word for "water." When Trudeau was elected, he cried a lot, and he also made many promises to Indigenous Nations and Indigenous Peoples that he never upheld. I envisioned a boxed water made from Trudeau's tears—would you drink that?

On the first night of the show, I displayed the Trud'eau boxes out in the lobby in my Candy Girl Stand. I gave a few of the boxes away as souvenirs to some people from the Indigenous community. When it was showtime, I ended up leaving the boxes in the lobby while we were on stage. When I came back to the lobby after the show, I discovered that people had taken some of the boxes. It was an interesting exercise in trust; I wonder who took the boxes? Why they took the boxes, and if they thought that it was okay that they just took something that was just sitting there. It seemed typical. Indians have something really cool; we turn our back for a second, and other people steal it.

Encounters at the 'Edge of the Woods'

THE PLAY AND ITS AFTERMATH

THE COLLECTIVE ENCOUNTER WITH JILL CARTER

Indigenous Company Members

Jenny Blackbird (nehiyaw): Installation Artist & Performer
Candy Blair (Mohawk): Performer
Jill Carter (Anishinaabe): Director & Dramaturg
Melanie Laking (Anishinaabe): Performer
Lee Maracle (Stó:lō): Storyteller
Trina Moyan (nehiyaw): Performer
Jennifer Alicia Murrin (L'nu): Performer
Natasha Naveau (Anishinaabe): Videographer & Projection Artist
Pesch Nepoose (nehiyaw): Performer
Brenda Wastasecoot (nehiyaw): Performer

Non-Indigenous Company Members

Abdul Mannan Ahmad: Performer
Susan Aaron: Sound Collector
Nicole Eun Jun Bell: Set Designer & Projection Designer
Sherry Bie: Installation Artist
Katia Café-Febrissy: Performer
Cayla Clarkson: Stage Manager
Megan Davies: Assistant Stage Manager
Max Frearon: Performer
Andrew Kesik: Performer
Isabel Klassen-Marshall: Transcriber & Costume Co-ordinator
Lauren Lacey: Assistant Lighting Designer
Uri Livne-Bar: Performer & Sound Designer
Sharai Masanganise: Performer
Sarah Michaels: Performer
Grace Phan: Performer
Sheilah Salvador: Performer

Tushita (Tuhi) Sen: Performer
Gabriele Simmons: Installation Artist
Shirka Urechko: Sound Designer
Hallie Wells: Performer

SCENE ONE

FALSE START

WATER SINGERS enter the theatre and begin to gather onstage. They are preparing to rehearse Nibi (Water) Song. CANDY GIRL (The Trickster-Usher) enters through the house. Dressed and carefully coiffed, she presents as an edgy, acerbic Betty Boop. She wears a cigarette tray from which she has been selling "Trud'eau" boxed water distilled from 150 years of Indigenous tears.

CANDY GIRL: *(as she travels through the house)* CELL PHONES OFF, PLEASE! TURN OFF YOUR CELL PHONES! CELL PHONES OFF, PLEASE! CELL PHONES OFF! THANK YOU!

CANDY GIRL ascends to the stage. The singers greet her, gather, and begin to sing Nibi (Water) Song,[1] *as a second company mounts the stage and prepares their own rehearsal: DIRECTOR, "HAMLET," "OPHELIA," STAGE MANAGER, and a MAKEUP ARTIST explode into the space. All are scrambling to keep up with the DIRECTOR. "OPHELIA" is in white-face and wears an over-size white gown or duster. She looks like a sad circus clown. "HAMLET" is heavily made up in the manner of a goth clown.*

DIRECTOR: She needs a wig! Find me a wig! My kingdom for a wig!

HAMLET: And a beard! I would like a beard, please!

MAKEUP ARTIST: She doesn't need a wig! Her hair looks great.

---

1 Nibi (Water) Song was written by Doreen Day after her grandson Mashkoonce expressed his wish to sing to the water in Ojibwemowin (the Ojibwe language). To hear this song, learn more about its creation, or learn the lyrics and melody, please visit The Mother Earth Water Walk website: http://www.motherearthwaterwalk.com/?attachment_id=2244.

DIRECTOR: Wig! Now! Blonde!

A COSTUMIER enters and shoves a monstrous blonde wig on OPHELIA's head.

Better.

HAMLET: My beard?

COSTUMIER: No beard today.

DIRECTOR: No beard. Hamlet doesn't have a beard.

HAMLET: But.

OPHELIA: Why do I have to wear this awful makeup?

MAKEUP ARTIST: Awful? I think you mean awesome.

HAMLET: That's right! Why this makeup? She doesn't need this crap!

MAKEUP ARTIST: Crap?!?

DIRECTOR: She does.

OPHELIA: I don't!

DIRECTOR: We need the makeup!

HAMLET: Why?

DIRECTOR: We need the makeup because Ophelia is white. Duh.

DIRECTOR notices WATER SINGERS.

Hey! Wrap it up! Time's up! Get off our stage!

PESCH: So rude!

STAGE MANAGER: I think they have five more minutes.

DIRECTOR: Off! Out!

BRENDA: Not until we are finished, young man.

CANDY: We have five more minutes!

They begin singing again.

STAGE MANAGER: I told you . . .

DIRECTOR: Wrap it up, girls! You have NO more minutes!

BRENDA: Show some respect! Wait your turn!

DIRECTOR: Move aside, Grandma. This is THEATRE! Not some Pow Wow. We're making art here.

STAGE MANAGER: They still have three . . .

ANDREW: OUT!

(to his company) PLACES, NOW!

As WATER SINGERS begin to leave, STAGE MANAGER tries to apologize to TRINA. She ignores him. The MAKEUP ARTIST is trying to flirt with PESCH, who runs away. The WATER SINGERS exit through the audience towards the lobby.

DIRECTOR: FUUUUUUUCK!!!

The COSTUMIER, who has been trying to adjust OPHELIA's wig so that it looks somewhat presentable, exits disgustedly, followed by the MAKEUP ARTIST.

HAMLET: My beard! Hamlet needs a beard!

STAGE MANAGER: Where do you want to go from?

DIRECTOR: "I loved you not."

Hamlet, remember you are a like a cobra getting ready to strike! Strike at her heart!

STAGE MANAGER: Places, please! Act 3, scene 1. Nunnery. "I loved you not."

> *HAMLET and OPHELIA take their places.*

> *Faint sounds of water, now barely audible, rise steadily through the scene.*

HAMLET: I loved you not.

DIRECTOR: STRIKE!

HAMLET: I LOVED YOU NOT!

OPHELIA: I was the more deceived.

DIRECTOR: Damn right, bitch.

HAMLET: Get thee to a nunnery.

Why wouldst thou be a breeder of sinners? I am myself indifferent, honest, but yet I could accuse me of such things that it were better my mother had not borne me: I am very proud, revengeful, ambitious, with more offenses at my beck than I have thoughts to put them in, imagination to give them shape, or time to act them in. What should such fellows as I do crawling between earth and heaven? We are arrant knaves all; believe none of us. Go thy ways to a nunnery. Where's your father?

DIRECTOR: Move into her! What's your intention here? What are you saying to her? Really saying? Get thee to a nunnery, BITCH! Why are you such a fucking WHORE? I'm just an average guy—no worse than most, but I am capable of horrible things. MOVE IN HERE! LET THE SERPENT IN YOUR PANTS START TO UNCOIL! LET IT SWELL—"I have thoughts." What thoughts? What do you want to do to this bitch?

HAMLET: Okay. Serpent in my pants.

Get thee to a nunnery. Why wouldst thou be a breeder of sinners? I am myself indifferent, honest, but yet I could accuse me of such things that it were better my mother had not borne me: I am very proud, revengeful, ambitious, with more offenses at my beck than I have thoughts to put them in, imagination to give them shape, or time to act them in.

DIRECTOR: Grab her throat!

> *HAMLET does this half-heartedly.*

Like you mean it! This bitch just broke up with you! She betrayed you! BETRAYED! Like your whore-mother betrayed your father. You've had it! You're done! No more Mr. Nice Guy! No more bitches! Your uncle killed your father. Your mother is fucking your father's murderer. Your girlfriend is giving it away to everybody in the kingdom except you—bitches and whores. Bitches and whores. You're surrounded by bitches and whores!!!

> *DIRECTOR moves in to strike OPHELIA. As he raises his arm, we hear the sound of a railway spike. All freeze, as the sounds of water increase in volume and intensity.*

> *The WATER SINGERS, who have remained in the house, begin to sing Nibi (Water) Song. Their song rises in volume and power with the water.*

OPHELIA: What's that noise?

DIRECTOR: Places! "I loved you not!"

HAMLET and OPHELIA take their places—visibly nervous.

WOMAN runs in through the house.

WOMAN: EVERYBODY OUT! NOW! FLOOD! TADDLE CREEK IS FLOODING THE THEATRE!

DIRECTOR: I thought we buried that sewer in 1884!

STAGE MANAGER: We did.

Song and water continue to rise in volume. All freeze on stage except for STAGE MANAGER, who finds a spotlight front off-centre.

Interestingly, 1884 was also the year when they amended the Indian Act to ban all Indigenous ceremony. Songs. Dances. Regalia.

DIRECTOR: FUUUUCK! Who cares! We open in a few hours!

WOMAN: Uh, I doubt that.

TRINA: The water has been assaulted.

BRENDA: You have offended a living relative.

JENNIFER: Your offenses will not stay buried.

DIRECTOR: SHUT UP! STUPID WATER! STUPID BITCHES!

WATER SINGERS increase their volume. Chaos.

COSTUMIER and MAKEUP ARTIST run in from backstage.

COSTUMIER: There's water everywhere! The dressing rooms are flooded!

HAMLET and OPHELIA try to run backstage to save their stuff. We see them choking on the stench emanating from the filthy floodwaters backstage.

CANDY: Violated treaties!

PESCH: Violated women!

BRENDA: Violated children!

JENNY: Violated land!

CANDY: Theft!

BRENDA: Lies!

JENNIFER: Prevarications!

WOMAN: We have to get out!

OPHELIA, HAMLET, COSTUMIER, and MAKEUP ARTIST run down, forming a line and freezing in tableau on the lip of the stage. DIRECTOR has circled upstage. STAGE MANAGER is caught between trying to escape the deluge and coaxing ANDREW to safety.

DIRECTOR: NO! Act 3, scene 1. "I loved you not!" Places. Now!

The show must go on!

Silence. Hamlet company freezes. Water sounds.

WATER PROTECTORS walk down two aisles of the house towards the stage.

TRINA: No. It has gone on long enough. This is over.

CANDY: This is over.

PESCH: This is over.

JENNY: This is over.

JENNIFER: This is over.

MELANIE: This is over.

They reach the front and mount the stage. BRENDA *gently reaches out to touch the* DIRECTOR.

BRENDA: This is over.

Projection: In 1884, the Indian Act was amended to prohibit all expressions of Indigenous ceremony across these territories now commonly referred to as "Canada." THIS *was also the year in which plans were set in motion and contracts were ratified to activate the final burial of Ziibiinehse (Taddle Creek). In 2004, Ziibiinehse was breached during elevator construction at Hart House. The theatre was closed for three months.* Hamlet *was cancelled.*

The projection dissolves "in water," merging into a projection of Lee Maracle telling a traditional story about the Double-Headed Serpent on Turtle Island.

SCENE TWO

DOUBLE-HEADED SERPENT: PART ONE[2]

LEE: *(projected)* I'm going to tell my version of this story. Back home where we come from, we say we work with story. We have kept versions, which are very short. And then we tell our own versions, which are mythmaking because someone needs to hear something that is contained in this story. I'm going to tell one that I know I have told before in the Longhouse—and I know I have told before at an Indian college, and I have told to my children and nieces and nephews many times so that they could learn something from the story. I do know the kept version, but we don't tell that in a crowd, and we don't tell it on machines. Instead, we work with the story. This story is very old. This story took place in the time of the flood. When the waters started to recede and the women started to come down the mountains and rebuild their lives and the men started to return in their boats, they started to rebuild their society, but the flood had been such a terrible, terrible murderous affair. Many, many animals died. Fishes died. Whales' carcasses were everywhere. And many human beings died. And the people were terrified. And terrified people can't be trusted.

When people are terrified, they have bad thoughts. When people are terrified, they make up—fiction up—stories about how this might have happened, and they're usually not on target. They're usually not right. Our imagination gets carried away. And soon we're angry with one another, instead of angry at what happened.

2 Lee Maracle's entire oration will not be documented in this script. We have chosen to publish the first part that you read here because this portion of Lee's telling was made publicly available on a livestreamed version of *Streaming Life: Storying the 94*, a land-based truth activation, conceived by Jill Carter, written and performed by members of the Collective Encounter and the "Deep Time" academic working group. It was directed in 2021 by Jill Carter with Antje Budde. *Streaming Life: Storying the 94* is available on YouTube at https://www.youtube.com/watch?v=VxEpi0noKLU. The remainder of Lee Maracle's oration will be summarized throughout this script.

So many people died; so many people, they could not be grieved. They could not hold ceremony. They could not be properly interred. And so, their descendants are angry at other people who are responsible for taking care of their dead.

And eventually wars broke out. Men went to war against other men. And villages fought other villages. And that woke up the Double-Headed Serpent who is always hungry. The serpent has two heads. One head wants the conscience of the people, and the other head wants to solve its problems. And the only way that they can live among the people is to share moments in which the hungry head gets to eat what he wants, and the loyal head gets to eat what he wants. And at first, they were fighting each other. But eventually they realized that if they fought each other, both would die. And that would be a terrible waste. So, they took turns swallowing people's spirits. The hungry people, the angry people—they would swallow their conscience. And eventually they became warriors without conscience.

And they started to kill small children. They started to kill women. And the women had to hide in the bushes, hide from the serpent and hide from the men that were going to war against them.

Eventually, a small boy said to his mother, "I'm going to kill that serpent; he's got our people killing each other."

SCENE THREE

SPLIT MIND OVERTURE

TRINA: My two brains are spinning, rolling, rolling, spinning inside my skulls.

BRENDA: His eyes are very familiar.

PESCH: The serpents are guarding Taddle Creek.

BRENDA: My grandson is very brave.

JENNIFER: Mouths agape; tongues aflame.

BRENDA: He's always talking about scary things.

CANDY: Water swallows pain;

Cools the nightmare-sweats

INDIGENOUS CAST: He has seen this place before.

MAX: We hold the memories like precious water;
Yet, it drips through our fingers,

SHARAI: Water trickles into our minds,

GRACE: Vissssscoussssss!

URI: "Oh mighty streamlet! All who have known thee
have learned of thee and loved thee.

ANDREW: Except the Board of Health!"

NON-INDIGENOUS CAST laughs uproariously. Then falls silent in realization.

SHEILAH: Watching in horror
When we realize that we can't change the shape of our hands.

INDIGENOUS CAST: Wiitigo![3] *(echoing)*

SARAH: The dark clouds gathering upon the hills foretell floods that might end the lives of the earthbound creatures.

MANNAN: The lions and the bears are terrified too.

CANDY GIRL: *(to audience)* "This is an uncomfortable day for Canada, but it is an essential day."

JENNIFER: You should probably
Talk less
Listen more
(to audience) Dropping one show in a century of seasons does not count.
If I don't see actions, I don't digest words.
We don't need your sympathy
Or your guilt.
Emotional labour is not our responsibility.
To engage in your decolonization process
There are no excuses
Keystone
Kinder Morgan
Enbridge Line 3
You can google this shit
You can start by acknowledging this is Indigenous land.

---

3 A spectre of unassuageable hunger, Wiitigo/Wendigo has been known for centuries by the Algonquin-speaking peoples as a cannibalistic spirit, which would enter a village and consume all living creatures within its environs, and which would finally turn upon itself when there was no more prey to be eaten. Professor Weetahgo (who appears later in this play) is Wiitigo in human face.

BRENDA: All of it.

PESCH: All of it.

CANDY: All of it.

TRINA: All of it.

MELANIE: All of it.

JENNIFER: All of it.

BRENDA: For ONE HUNDRED AND FIFTY YEARS!
They raped the land.

INDIGENOUS CAST: Wiitigo *(repeated echoes)*

BRENDA: Laid their railway and drove in that last gold spike.
This was not just one dark chapter;
This is the whole story.

KATIA: I'm sorry.

MAX: Don't put it on me.

BRENDA: Still, some say it never happened.

KATIA: The spirit of our oppressed people is still here, bubbling up. The beauty of the tree is only there to cover our wrongdoings. Bodies are upside down; cores, stitched back together; parts of animals, mutilated.

INDIGENOUS CAST does "Wiitigo Teeth."

The tree is not brown. It is *grey*!
The colour of terror.

SHARAI: Is this healing or encountering? Is the past voice being heard, shared as a story?

KATIA: It's as if these bodies were petrified in cement.
I hear cries; I hear screams; I smell their last breath.

URI: I'm sorry.

ANDREW: Don't put it on me.

PESCH: That happens a lot to you Natives. Right?
In your reserves and communities. It happens lots in your community, right? Drugs and alcohol and violence.

KATIA: I'm sorry.

MAX: Don't put it on me.

SHEILAH: If you can't find a safe space,

GRACE: Carve yourself a brave space

KATIA: Reason versus desire.

ANDREW: Have to versus want to.

JENNIFER M: Yes, this is another NDN poem.

L'nu na niin
Because a white farmer gets away with murdering a young Indigenous man,
Because the response is "we have to do better,"
Because the not guilty verdict was determined by an all-white jury.

ANDREW: Cite your sources!

JENNIFER: I will continue to fight
Until all of us are water protectors
Until we are no longer protestors
Civil disobedients.
Trespassers on our own land?
Savages
Stereotypes
A chapter in a textbook
A lesson plan
Historical
As in no longer here
As in we don't exist
As if we aren't the original caretakers of this land.
They step over us
While telling us to get over it
As if Canada wasn't founded on geno—

All gasp in horror and freeze; JENNIFER *claps a hand over her mouth.*

SHEILAH: OOOOH! Say my name!

ANDREW: How do strangers become friends?

SHEILAH: Say my name!

Awkward pause.

PESCH: Once I sat on an edge like this before.

MELANIE: Two Row

MAX: Once I sat on an edge like this before.

TRINA: Royal Proclamation

GRACE: Once I sat on an edge like this before.

CANDY: Treaty of Niagara

PESCH: Batoche

MELANIE: Treaty 13

MANNAN: Toronto Purchase

JENNIFER: 1787. BLANK

ANDREW: Signed by your chiefs!

TRINA: With glued-on clan symbols!

ANDREW: 1805

MELANIE: Ten shillings

ANDREW: Sold!

CANDY: It was treaty!

MELANIE: An agreement to share!

TRINA: Indian Act . . .

PESCH: White Paper . . .

BRENDA: The Sixties Scoop . . .

MELANIE: Oka . . .

PESCH: Ipperwash . . .

CANDY: Standing Rock . . .

BRENDA: Chemical Valley . . .

CANDY: Missing and Murdered . . .

JENNIFER: You can google this shit.

KATIA: I'm sorry!

MAX: Don't put it on me.

Awkward pause.

URI: Once I sat on an edge like this before.

SHARAI: Is this healing or encountering? Is the past voice being heard, shared as a story?

SARAH: It's not the first time this happens
But it is the first time I actually feel a connection.

TUHI: Winding path
Throbbing drums
Ceremony
Deep booming voices
Echoes
Fire
Insistence
Smoke
Ashes
I perish in my own flames,
to the rhythm of the throbbing drums
and the rattle of the shaking earth

All form circle of protection around TUHI.

SARAH: Compassion pooling in your eyes
As you watch my body
Share the story of my vulnerability
Which I didn't want to tell today.

PESCH: I'm so glad I worked at that hellhole for six months.

CANDY: 'Cause then I got to meet you!

PESCH: See? Everything happens for a reason.

All gesture.

KATIA: This whole time has felt like a loose tooth that is being yanked slowly, very slowly until the root has started to show. We are apart; yet so together.

NON-INDIGENOUS CAST falls back into irreconcilable space.

TRINA: I am the split-minded serpent rising up from my mother's heart.

MELANIE: Petroglyphs.

CANDY: Teaching Rocks

PESCH: The serpents are guarding Ziibiinehse.

JENNIFER: Mouths agape; tongues aflame

TRINA: The two-leggeds surrender to the ancient knowledge.

Projection: LEE Maracle (on screen) speaks about ethical witnessing and about working with traditional story.

CANDY: Need peace, miss peace
Culture
Longhouse, Longhouse, Longhouse
Dance
Corn husk baskets and dolls
Picking beans, nuts, corn.
Singing with family at night
Speaking Kanien'kéha

CANDY MELANIE: Anishinaabemowin

TRINA BRENDA: nehiyawewin

CANDY: Tears, tears, tears.

PESCH: Excuses, excuses, excuses.

CANDY: It's not fair.

MANNAN: I'm sorry.

SHEILAH: Don't put it on me.

ANDREW: How do strangers become friends?

NON-INDIGENOUS CAST: Friends? Friends? Friends?

Both casts fade back to irreconcilable space. Blackout.

In the darkness, we hear:

SARAH: Once upon a dream,
there was a magical waterfall where bears were lions,
and lions breathed fire into bears.

PESCH: Where Sun and Moon created one whole.

JENNIFER: Where Moon cared for the water and tugged on our wombs.

MELANIE: Where Sun feasted Aki (earth) and thawed frozen hearts.

CANDY: Need peace, miss peace.

We hear the slow, deliberate click of high heels.

SCENE FOUR

PROFESSOR WEETAHGO: INTERNATIONAL DIPLOMACY—TREATIES 101

PROFESSOR WEETAHGO is a beautiful, confident university professor. She is dressed in designer fashion and "killer" heels. Whenever she appears, the theatre is transformed into a lecture hall. She is a nehiyaw woman who has paid dearly for her success in her chosen occupation; unfortunately, she is now "Wiitigo," and she has already begun consuming herself. Hence, her arm (now gnawed down to a bloody stump) is heavily bandaged and remains an irresistible temptation to her. While lecturing, WEETAHGO succumbs to her cravings, and as her lecture continues throughout the play, the frequency of her "snacking" increases.

WEETAHGO: Congratulations! You are the lucky few who have made it into my course. I am Professor Weetahgo, and this is International Diplomacy: Treaties 101.

She snarls.

Oh! Pardon me. I skipped lunch. SLIDE!

You, back there. Yeah, you! Close the doors. They lock automatically. Which brings us to rule number one. Never, never, never, never be late for my class. If you know you are going to be late, don't bother coming. Ever.

Oh, look! Someone's at the door now! Yeah!

She smiles, waves, gestures, dismisses.

You're not getting in today, or ever again.

Alright! So, rule number two. My books. I'm sure you noted in the syllabus that I have authored ten books. And all of them will be used throughout this course. And you are expected to purchase all ten. They're a little pricey, but I've worked hard, and I deserve my royalties. If you can't afford them, that's not my problem. Get a loan or call *mommy and daddy*. Maybe they'll help you.

Rule number three I never ever, *ever* offer extensions because I believe extensions engender weakness. Weakness is not tolerated in this class.

Finally, I am proud to tell you that in my fifteen years of teaching at this institution, I have never granted an A+. And I'm not about to start now. Not with the likes of you.

She snarls.

Although you may try to tempt me.

As I'm sure you are all aware, this is Canada's largest institution! It's ranked twentieth in the world. Do you know what that means? It means that you are here to compete. But please go ahead! Turn to the person beside you. Say "hello." Oh, Hi! Hello! Hi there!

Stop! I said, STOP! That is not your friend. That's your competition! I grade on a bell curve, and it's eat or be eaten in this course. *MMMMMM.*

What next? Ah, yes! Indigenous "content"! SLIDE!

In accordance with the report you are reading on this slide, our course must include Indigenous content. Therefore, our first class is entirely devoted to Indigenous treaty-making in this region. Personally, I have questions about this. SLIDE!

As my good friends Frances Widdowson and Albert Howard have observed in their seminal book *Disrobing the Aboriginal Industry:*

(reads from slide) "The demand of Native control over curriculum assures that traditional cultural practices have precedence over modern communication requirements so that students remain unprepared for the disciplines of secondary education. The secondary schools are then adjusted to allow Aboriginal Peoples to graduate artificially. And why stop there? Many undergraduate programs are now specifically designed for Natives, where the application of 'Aboriginal' signifies the lower standard of the degree."[4]

But take it from me, this is no "bird course." Birdies don't survive here.

She snarls.

OKAY! Land Acknowledgement.

(reading from cellphone) "We wish to acknowledge this land on which the University of Toronto operates. For thousands of years."

A Barry White ringtone signals an incoming call.

It's my publisher. Excuse me! I have to take this. In the meantime, please watch this carefully and be prepared to discuss.

Projection: Melanie Laking's Land Acknowledgement. In the gloom, off to the side, we can see WEETAHGO *gesticulating as she speaks animatedly into her phone.*

MELANIE: *(projection)* Aanii. Melanie indizhinikaaz. Anishinaabekwe indaaw. Shawanaga indoonjibaa. Giigoonh indoodem. Aaniish ezhinikaazoyin? What is your name? Do you prefer to be called aki? Is gitigaan your name? I offer you my most sincere apology for taking three years to properly introduce myself. It was terrible behavior, and I

4 Widdowson, Frances, and Albert Howard. *Disrobing the Aboriginal Industry: The Deception Behind Indigenous Cultural Preservation*. McGill-Queen's University Press, 2008. 193.

am sorry. Please accept this semaa. I want to enter into good relations with you. I want to help you thrive.

I commit to learning the true names of everyone you share yourself with as a sign of my respect and good intentions. I will teach these names to my children and work to replace the Zhaganaashiimowin imposters until your true names roll easily off our tongues. I promise to rid you of the strange green grass and reunite you with the plant beings that you have known for time immemorial. Indigenous pollinator plants will bring the memengwenyig back and keep the gchi ahmook happy. I have a growing list of plants that I hope will please you. I am saving up for a rain barrel. This summer is supposed to be a hot one and collecting nibi from the sky will help quench your thirst.

The video fades out. A lecture slide replaces it: five bullet points critique Indigenous views of land and relationship. Lights up on WEETAHGO.

WEETAHGO: And we're back! Melanie n'dish nnnnuh nnnnish Nish Dish provides an interesting window into the ways in which our Indigenous People still think. She speaks to the land as if it could understand her and answer her questions! "What is your name?" She apologizes to the land for her "bad behavior," and commits herself to a series of actions to atone for that behavior and repair their fractured "relationship"! Through her performance, Nish Dish demonstrates the quaint notion of the land as a treaty partner, which must be appeased with gifts.

WEETAHGO *cackles.*

Interspecies diplomacy in action!!

Lights down on WEETAHGO. *Lights up on* MELANIE *Laking, who replaces her video-self and carries on with her Land Acknowledgement.*

MELANIE: Miigwetch for giving my children a safe place to play. I am grateful to you for not holding my poor behaviour against them. They have never been stung by an ahmoo while in your care nor cut by the sharp leaves of the mitig that reaches over you. Miigwetch for accepting my family into the biota that you sustain. Adding more of us to your care must be difficult. I know that you are tired.

Lights down on MELANIE *and up on* WEETAHGO.

WEETAHGO: "I know that you are tired"! No, don't laugh. This is not a joke. This is *Interspecies diplomacy*! Live up to your contractual obligations or else! Buzzzzzz!

WEETAHGO *mimes being stung by a bee.*

Ack! SLIDE!

Nishnabick scholar Leanne Simpson explains:

(reading slide) "In many instances, clan leaders negotiated particular agreements with animal nations or clans to promote *(mispronouncing)* Bimaadiziwin and balance with the region. In Mississauga territory, for example, the people of the fish clans, who are the intellectuals of the nation, met with the fish nations twice a year for thousands of years at [M-n-in—Mim-Minnn]"—up north somewhere.[5]

(with great authority) I believe Melanie Nish Dish also identifies herself as a member of the Fish-Dodo. So, every year, Nish Dish and her Nishnabick pals get together to talk treaties with the fish. AAACK!

5 Simpson, Leanne. "Looking after Gdoo-naaganinaa: Precolonial Nishnaabeg Diplomatic and Treaty Relationships." *Wicazo Sa Review* (23, 2): Fall 2008. 29–42.

SCENE FIVE

BRENDA WASTASECOOT DELIVERS HER LECTURE

Lights down on WEETAHGO *and up on* BRENDA. *Projections behind* BRENDA *move silently and very rapidly. Scenes of drilling, mining, extraction. Scenes of clear-cut forests. Images of polluted water. Images of construction. Atlas Dewatering in Philosophers' Walk? Headlines:* MMIGW.

BRENDA: For ONE HUNDRED AND FIFTY YEARS!
They took our brothers and sisters
On the Train of Tears
To the schools far away.
I felt their pain when I was five
When I was left behind
To pick up the pieces
Of broken windows
And broken hearts.

For ONE HUNDRED AND FIFTY YEARS!
They removed our brothers and sisters
From their mothers' embraces
From their communities
From their culture and language.
I saw the pain in their faces
And in my mother's eyes
In the letters my father wrote to his children
Sending ten hugs and ten kisses.

For ONE HUNDRED AND FIFTY YEARS!
They raped the land
Laid their railway and drove in that last gold spike.
This was not just one dark chapter
This is the whole story
THIS IS THE WHOLE STORY!

Beat.

Still, some say it never happened
And nonbelievers didn't teach their children
The true history of this land
Called Canada.

Blackout. In the blackout we hear:

WEETAHGO: Some call it rape; I call it *development*.
Tomato, tomahto. Potato, potahto.

SCENE SIX

VIOLENCE-WEAVE

GRAY: What happens to me happens to you.

MAX: What happens to you happens to me.

GRAY: It was a housewarming party in Scarborough and everyone else lived very far away, but I just lived down the street. And because they lived so far away, they had to leave.

MAX: Take me with you.

GRAY: But I stayed behind because I wasn't afraid of not getting home safely. But I should've left with everyone else. Because I didn't feel safe sitting on that couch.

GRAY gestures.

MAX: This is normal; this is normal; this is normal.

GRAY: The person turned into a presence. And it wasn't the size that was terrifying; it was how it felt. It was viscous.

CAST: Vissssoussssss ssssss. Viscoussss sssss. *(echoed throughout)*

CANDY: I don't like this place

GRAY: And it seeped through all the threads of your shirt and filled your pores

KATIA: Sssssssstinks reeeeeeks of bad smells . . . of murders

MAX: Smoke

CAST: Visssscousssssssssssss

GRAY: It was so hard to breathe. And then it told me to get up and walk to the bedroom

From offstage comes banging and loud voices.

MAX: I breathe, and I try to remind myself that this is normal, this is normal, this is normal. I've never met my neighbour, but he always has strange visitors at night. Sometimes banging on doors, sometimes mine. Maybe they get the unit number wrong? I don't know

Banging and loud voices.

MAX: Louder, louder, their voices remind me of a different voice. And there's a weight on my chest, spreads down to my stomach. Down to my legs, like someone on top of me. A gentler voice, a voice that made me feel powerless

GRAY: It robbed me of who I thought I was supposed to be. And I can't wash that away

MAX: Powerless.

CAST: *(hisses and breathes)* sssssssss

GRAY: I couldn't move back because the presence was there. And if I went forward, it would trail along behind me.

MAX: All is quiet, for just a moment, and then BAAAAAA!!! BAAAAA!!! *This* is not normal.

CAST: BAAAA! BAAAA! BAAAA!!

GRAY: I couldn't move back because the presence was there.

CAST: BAAAA! BAAA! BAAA!!

MAX: *This* is not normal. The fire alarms are going off throughout the building. It's three in the morning! I grab my keys, my shoes, and my *knife*.

GRAY: *This* is not normal!

MAX: My small silver pocketknife, the one I carry to make sure that no one can make me feel powerless again.

Pause.

And the alarms are BAAAA.

CAST: BAAA! BAAAA! BAAAA!

MAX: But the voices are quiet.

GRAY: Shhhhh.

MAX: I reach for the door . . .

GRAY: Take me with you!

MAX: I reach for the door!

Reaching. Frozen with indecision.

Where are the men? And their voices? Why were they banging on my door? What do they want? Was it a lure? Do they want me to come out? Me? All alone in this big apartment? I'm standing there, and every fiber of my body wants to go back to bed and pretend like this is normal.

Pause.

Smoke, smoke!

CAST: *(hisses and breathes)* Sssssssssssss

GRAY: And if I went forward, it would trail along behind me. And when I was on that bed, it wasn't behind me, but it was everywhere and on top of me. And I was in an ocean of cotton, sweat, and aftershave.

CAST: Sssssssssssssss

MAX: And there's a weight on my chest.

GRAY: And the presence, it pushed me into the bed.
And it kept going back and forth, back and forth, back and forth.
It took. It *robbed* me of who I thought I was supposed to be. And I can't wash that away.

> *Lights up on* WEETAHGO, *who has been watching this scene and who now continues her lecture.*

WEETAHGO: So, if we follow this line of thinking through to its *illogical* conclusion, we can see why the Nishnabick and our other Indigenous friends continue to act out and block economic progress. Earth is Mother. And resource extraction equals violence on Mother. Equals rape. Equals a breakdown of social relations. Equals violence on other human bodies.

> WEETAHGO *laughs at these ridiculous ideas.*

> *Lights down on* WEETAHGO.

MAX: I'm looking at the door.

GRAY: Take me with you!

MAX: And I'm not scared of the fire; I'm scared that there isn't one.

WEETAHGO: Okay! Moving on! Two Row Wampum 1613. SLIDE!

SCENE SEVEN

WEETAHGO MOVES ON

Lights up on WEETAHGO, *who continues to lecture in front of a projection of the Two Row Wampum as if no interruption had occurred.*

WEETAHGO: *(referring to the projection behind her)* A "treaty" ratified between the Dutch and the Hod—Hhhaud—Iroquois. This bunch of beads was replicated and exchanged between multiple nations throughout the era of early settlement. The purple row of beads on top represents the European *discoverers* sailing along in their ship—

She demonstrates majestic sailing.

—while the Indigenous Peoples on the bottom paddle their canoe.

She demonstrates paddling.

Our Indigenous Peoples consider this to be a treaty ratified between two sovereign nations—an agreement to share these lands and to not interfere with or impede the progress of the other.

A quaint notion, but of course, completely *unworkable*. Treaty?! NOT! But nice workmanship! A lovely collector's item and a great investment if you can get your hands on one. SLIDE!

Projection: Dish with One Spoon Wampum.

Another attempt at treaty-making by our primitive—uh, *Indigenous* friends. This bunch of beads was also replicated and exchanged repeatedly throughout the SEVENTEENTH, EIGHTEENTH, and NINETEENTH centuries. It represents an agreement between the Nishnabick of Mississauga and the Iroquois who controlled this area. A very strategic area, may I say. A corridor through which goods and people have always flowed back and forth. Back and forth.

She gestures.

And an area rich in resources. Anyway, they agreed to share the contents of this "dish"—this *land*—amongst each other equally, making sure that no individual took too much, and no individual went without.

Let me remind you here of Melanie Nish Dish and Leanne Simpson! This "treaty" also is *supposed* to include all the rocks, and trees, and birds, and fish, and animals *as treaty partners*!

She dissolves into laughter.

But really, it's not a bad attempt—considering they had no alphabet!

Seriously, though. I put it to *you*: Could such an agreement work in today's complex world? Any ideas? How would *you* put this into action?

She looks out into audience. The audience lights go up. She waits for a response.

If there is no response: "I didn't think so. Moving on!"

If there is a response: "You have an idea you would like to share? Moving on!"

The Toronto Purchase. Now, *this* is interesting. The British purchased this land—yes, *this* land—in 1787. They gave the Nishnabick some money, two thousand gun flints (maybe they should have rethought that one), twenty-four brass kettles, one bale of flowered flannel, TWENTY-FOUR lace hats, NINETY-SIX gallons of rum, and 120 mirrors in exchange for some 250,000 acres of land! One-hundred-and-twenty mirrors! Imagine! They had likely never seen themselves before! Bleecchhhh!

She laughs charmingly.

All of this is to say, that this was a purchase—fair and square. *Not* a treaty as some of our Indigenous malcontents now claim! And later, in 1805, the British gave them even more money! TEN shillings! The Nishnabick took the payment. They knew what they were selling. And we have the proof! The deed of sale. With their clan signatures.

GLUUUUU.

Uh.

With their clan signatures. Slide!

Projection: Toronto Purchase 1787—blank with Mississauga clan-symbols "wafered" on.

Ooops!

NEXT SLIDE!

SCENE EIGHT

TESTIMONY: THE MISSION SCHOOL

INDIGENOUS CAST and KATIA and SHEILAH witness on stage.

SHARAI : It began when I was five years old.

WITNESSES: She was only five years old. She was only five years old. *(echoes)*

TRINA: I had to pee.

SHARAI: Every night, I would call out in our room, "Does anybody want to go to the washroom with me?"

WITNESSES: Shhhh! Shhhh!

SHARAI: Anybody?

WITNESSES: Shhhh! Shhhh!

SHARAI: Washroom?

WITNESSES: Shhhh! Shhhh!

SHARAI: When no one did, I had to go alone.

The soundscape begins.

More than 100 metres in the dark, outside, to the latrines.
Afraid of the white ghosts.

WITNESSES: White ghostsssss. Ancestorssssss. Powerlessssss. Stinkssssss. Reeeeksssss. *(echoes)*

Projection: Front of residential school.

SHARAI: Tears flowing as I tiptoed.
Stars shining down.
Crickets singing.
Afraid and desperate, I would reach the blocks and search for a clean cubicle.

JENNIFER: It's stinky in here.

BRENDA: I don't like this place.

TRINA: I had to pee.

SHARAI: Always overflowing with filth and faeces.

PESCH: Everything happens for a reason.

BRENDA: FOR 150 YEARS.

SHARAI: Education.
Education as I experienced it.
Years back.
Memories now as new as today.

WITNESSES: FOR 150 YEARS.

SHARAI: Is this healing or encountering.?
Is the past being heard and shared as a story?

Do you hear me? Are we connected?
Why are your eyes drifting away from me?
Is the knowledge we gained at those mission schools worth the price we paid to know?

The WITNESSES *repeat Call and Response:*

WITNESSES: For 150 years.
Worth the price?
For 150 years.
Worth the price?

SCENE NINE

TESTIMONY: THE TRAIN OF TEARS

SHARAI: It began when I was five years old.

BRENDA: I am five years old, and something is happening!

WITNESSES: Something is happening! *(echoes)*

BRENDA: My brothers and sisters are running around.

They are in a hurry.
Ironing clothes. Packing suitcases.
They are speaking *English*!

MELANIE: Zhaagaanashaamowin.

PESCH: *English!*

BRENDA: They are leaving again.

PESCH: Take me with you!

MELANIE: Take me with you!

WITNESSES: Take me with you!

BRENDA: But they are dressing me!
We are going somewhere together!

> *BRENDA allows herself to be "dressed." PESCH and MELANIE echo gestures.*

Leotards. Itchy. Pinching me!

Coat.

BRENDA buttons it up to the neck.

Bonnet.
My sister cracks her gum.

WITNESSES crack gum.

MMMM. Spearmint.

BRENDA smooths her own bonnet. BRENDA sees her sister's face in front of her. She holds this vision with her eyes.

I love my sister.

WITNESSES: I love my sister. *(echoes)*

BRENDA: I love my sister.

They're taking me with them!

And then we are at the train.

But *no.*

WITNESSES: Noooooo.

BRENDA is "pulled away" from the train. WITNESSES mirror her contortions.

BRENDA: The train's over there!
Where are we going?
We come to a door.
My brother bangs on it.
BANG, BANG, BANG, BANG.

She waits.

BANG, BANG, BANG, BANG.

She waits.

BANG, BANG, BANG, BANG!
Finally, it opens, and they push me in.

BRENDA "pushed" in. PESCH and MELANIE "pushed" in. WITNESSES "pushed" in.

Recording of BRENDA singing Patsy Cline's "Crazy."

Chrome table legs. Human legs. Chair legs.
Where are we?
Thick smoke stings my eyes.
It's *stinky* in here.

JENNIFER: It's stinky in here.

BRENDA: I don't like this place.

BRENDA turns to leave. She is blocked by WITNESSES.

Then I hear my auntie.
"Mariah! Kibebbeem owa!"

WITNESSES echo Cree Auntie. Drunken laughter.

They let go of my hands!
Where are my sisters?
Where are my sisters?
Where are my sisters?
Where are my sisters? Where are my sisters?

Then I see them.
Running for the train.
Leaving me behind.

We hear the train pull away; BRENDA *and* WITNESSES *watch until it "disappears."*

Every fuckin' September, they left for the residential school on that Train of Tears.

WITNESSES *form a circle of protection around* BRENDA. *Call and Response begins and carries us into the next scene.*

Every fuckin' September.

WITNESSES: Worth the price?

BRENDA: Every fuckin' September.

WITNESSES: Worth the price?

WITNESSES *exit.* BRENDA *left behind. Lights down on Train of Tears and up on* TUHI, *who sits on steps downstage right.* BRENDA *exits on* TUHI*'s first line.*

SCENE TEN

TESTIMONY: FRAUD AND COMPLACENCY

TUHI: It was a warm spring afternoon, and one of my best friends and I were making coffee at my place and getting ready to work out. And she asks me, "What are you doing? How's school going?" So, I tell her, "Oh, I'm taking this Indigenous Studies course and I'm learning so much and I'm so excited about it!" And I tell her cool facts like, "Oh did you know the Toronto Land Purchase of 1787 was basically a blank document with the clan symbols of the Indigenous Chiefs just glued onto an empty sheet of paper and made to seem like an official deed of sale?"

Funnily enough, a couple weeks ago I was at a cash counter at LCBO grabbing a bottle for my friend with his credit card when it got rejected and the lady snatched the card from me and harshly accused me of committing fraud. But how does that even compare to the Toronto "Purchase?" Would she react with just as much anger if confronted with the fact that this whole city is sitting on the bones of fraud? I mean, the only reason any settler, including the cash lady, has been able to live their life here at all is because of that fake deed. Cash lady and I are both benefitting from fraud that began centuries ago, but I guess only one of us knows it.

WEETAHGO: *(off stage)* SLIDE!

> *Light out on* TUHI. *Light up on* WEETAHGO, *who continues her lecture.*

SCENE ELEVEN

PROFESSOR WEETAHGO EXPLAINS THE DOCTRINES

Projection: Bullet points about the Doctrine of Discovery.

WEETAHGO: So, in 1986, the Nishnabick of Mississauga launched a land claim with the government of Canada. They pointed to some *minor* irregularities in the 1787 Toronto Purchase, threw the word "treaty" around, and whined that they hadn't received proper compensation for this land. Well, seriously! LEARN TO NEGOTIATE! THAT'S WHAT DIPLOMACY IS ALL ABOUT!

We didn't have to give them a penny for it! Not one mirror. Not one drop of rum! Under the Doctrines of Discovery and of Terra Nullius, Canada holds underlying title to all lands within its borders! That's the law! But this is Canada. And Canada is *nice*! So, in 2014, Canada gave those Nishnabick 145 million dollars to shut them up. DONE! SOLD! ALL SALES FINAL!

These Indigenous Peoples just don't seem to understand this! Use it or lose it! They weren't using what they had to its fullest potential. And they certainly were not conducting themselves in a civilized manner! Singing to the water! Talking to the fish! Throwing their tobacco all around!

THE DOCTRINES OF DISCOVERY.

Well, thank goodness we discovered this land when we did! Who knows what would have become of all these resources if civilization had not stepped in!

The Doctrines of Discovery evolved through a series of papal bulls dating back to the thirteenth century. Basically, some pope ruled that while the backward and barbarous do possess some natural rights, the lands they once occupied are ultimately owned by the civilized peoples who discover them. Yes. I know. Canada is a secular state. But we know how to take a good thing and develop it to suit the times. That's evolution! So, under Canadian law. . .

WITNESSES enter marching. They surround WEETAHGO, who is swept into their circle and marches with them, hollering to be heard.

. . . INDIGENOUS PEOPLES STILL HAVE A RIGHT TO LIVE ON OUR LAND AND TO SING TO THE WATER AND TALK TO THE FISH AND THROW THEIR TOBACCO AROUND, AS LONG AS THEY KEEP TO THEMSELVES AND DON'T OBSTRUCT THE BOUNDLESS POTENTIAL OF THE NATION THAT KEEPS THEM IN FRYBREAD!

BRENDA: Every fuckin' September.

WITNESSES: For 150 years.

The Call and Response repeats.

WEETAHGO: *Terra nullius?* Same concept. SLIDE!

WEETAHGO exits. WITNESSES continue to march and to call and respond. Their circle widens into the next scene. KATIA is now revealed in the centre of the circle.

SCENE TWELVE

TESTIMONY: "SINCE WHEN DO MONKEYS TALK?"

WITNESSES circle KATIA—marching.

BRENDA: Every fuckin' September.

WITNESSES: For 150 years.

Call and Response repeats until KATIA breaks it.

KATIA: I can't! I can't!
I can't stop washing my hands!
I am seven years old.

WITNESSES: She was only seven years old. Only seven years old!

Echoes repeat.

KATIA: It's my first day in a new school.
I walk to a desk.
Graciously.
I sit where I feel most comfortable.
In the first row.
The teacher starts the lesson. She's asking questions.
And I have got all the answers.

KATIA raises her hand and responds to questions, which we do not hear. She addresses an invisible educator somewhere in the audience.

Tipis?
Igloos!
1492!

Then comes recess.
Everybody is rushing through the door.
To run to the play yard.
I trail behind.
But I'm determined to make new friends.
I see a group of girls, and I make eye contact.
But they ignore me.

Gestural Cannon: WITNESSES *turn away from* KATIA *as she approaches them. Shadows appear on scrims. These are the bullies.*

KATIA: And then I see a group of boys.
They're calling me.
So, I go to them.
Victor is the leader.
With his large green eyes and his wiggly fingers.
They surround me.
I am alone in the middle of this circle
And I feel small.
Victor asks me to extend my hand
My right hand, my *writing* hand.
I do, thinking he's gonna shake it as a sign of friendship.
But at that moment
He starts snorting and *growling*
And as two boys hold my hand
Victor spits right in the centre of my palm
And says: "Since when do monkeys talk?
That's what you get for raising your hand in class!"
And all the other boys start going, "Hoo. Hoo. Hoo!"

SHADOWS: Hoo, hoo, hoo.

OFFSTAGE CAST: Hoo, hoo, hoo.

KATIA: The playground starts spinning.
I look at my hand.
It's still there.
Shaking like jelly!
I wipe my hand slowly on the concrete.
Hard.
Until it hurts.
And now.
I can't.
I can't.
I can't.
I can't!

Lights out on Testimony. Lights up on WEETAHGO.

SCENE THIRTEEN

PROFESSOR WEETAHGO EXPLAINS THE DOCTRINE OF TERRA NULLIUS

Projection: bullet-point facts outlining Terra Nullius.

WEETAHGO: The Indigenous Peoples were not properly conducting themselves; they were not using the land and resources to their fullest capacity. So, they don't deserve to control it! They don't deserve to share the resources either! The entrepreneurial *humans* who *discovered* this land were empowered by their enlightened spiritual leader to come and take what others were not using. And we are empowered under Canadian law to keep it!

PESCH: *(offstage)* Shut the fuck up. You don't know anything!

WEETAHGO: Use it or lose it! *That's the law.* Do you really want to be in a course where everybody gets an A? No! *You* want the A! *You* want to excel! *You* want to be boundless! Do you really want to live in a world where everybody drives a Hyundai—or worse, walks or takes the bus? No! You want your Beamer. You want your Ferrari! You want your Hermes, Louboutin, Chanel, Ferragamo, Versace, Burberry, McCartney! Don't you?!

You want to dance like nobody's watching! Sing like nobody can tell you to stop! Eat your steak without asking the cow's permission! Eat your steak, your veal, your lamb, your juicy, sizzling, scrumptious . . .

WIITIGO takes over. WEETAHGO loses control and becomes feral.

You want. You take. You want. You eat. Want. Take. Eat. Boundless.

Barry White announces an incoming call with an incessant ringtone. WIITIGO, who was once WEETAHGO, explores the source of the sound and begins to eat it.

INDIGENOUS CAST: Wiitigo! Wiitigo! *(echoes)*

WEETAHGO: Want! Take! Eat! Eat! Eat! Boundless!

As WEETAHGO *staggers upstage, she crosses paths with* MS. REDACTED, *who sashays downstage towards centre.* MS. REDACTED *blows kisses to* WEETAHGO *and to a projected photo of Prime Minister Justin Trudeau with heart hands over his heart.* WEETAHGO *sits on her upstage riser in shadow.*

SCENE FOURTEEN

FALSE START—TESTIMONY: MS. REDACTED

MS. REDACTED: *(imitates projection)* Justin and I,
Me and Justin,
We have a thing going on.

OFFSTAGE VOICES: I have to pee!

CANDY GIRL enters.

CANDY GIRL: ALL RIGHT, FOLKS! CELLPHONES ON! IT'S INTERMISSION!

MS. REDACTED flounces off.

Intermission.

SCENE FIFTEEN

TESTIMONY: MS. REDACTED

As audience members take their seats, MS. REDACTED *poses in frozen imitation of the projection behind her.* WEETAHGO *sits in shadow on her upstage riser.* CANDY *sits in shadow on stairs at stage left.* TUHI *sits in shadow on stairs at stage right.*

MS. REDACTED: Justin and I,
Me and Justin,
We have a thing going on.
But he pretends not to know me.
Justin!!! Baby!
Don't treat me like this.
I'm not like one of the others, those
women, those girls that went missing
between now and the '80s.
Don't think you can ghost me the way
the RCMP did their families, their babies.
I can ghost you harder with your predecessors,
your father's legacies.

Projection: past prime ministers in headdresses, face-paint, canoes, etc.

Bloodstains against your lead-free walls,
the music of phantom screams running
through your Ottawa Halls.
I can sink the pain of trauma and PTSD
so deep in your skin, it will last longer than the
Haida-inspired Raven on your left shoulder.

Maybe if you lick my lips, suck my tongue,
taste the mercury that flows in Grassy Narrows,
Slate Falls, that still oozes from the skins,

the blood of the Chippewas of Sarnia decades after Dryden.
Maybe if you make a “reservation” in one of my
low-class, no-star, third-world-rated trailers
in Cat Lake, the scent of black mould,
the fleas playing with your hair, and
the souls of angry children whispering
sweet nothings in your ear will keep you
hot and bothered all night long.
Then maybe, just maybe
YOU'LL REMEMBER MY NAME!

Let me wine and dine you
in one of my uninsulated,
non-ventilated kitchens,
powered by butane,
decorated with exposed
wires, ready to catch fire and
explode at any given second.
Feel what it's like to
drown in desperation and alcohol.
Choke on white flour, Klik, and
government cheese.
Get familiar
with the taste of poverty and diabetes.

Let me strip you down to
the bone, swallow your heart
leave you naked and scarred
afraid to answer the call of
your father's drums, to sway
to your mother's songs.
Let me ride you.

TRINA, CANDY, & TUHI: Yaaa! Yaaa! Yaaa!

They gesture.

SHEILAH: Tie you up and beat you
down. Feel the weight of oppression,
emasculation, and wrongful conviction
for at least seven generations.

Justin!
Baby!
Stop denying me.
Stop pretending you don't
know me.
I am not some
wham bam, thank you ma'am,
thank you for your fucking
donation kind of bitch!

Don't think you can
bamboozle, sweet talk, swindle
me like I am some kind of
Royal Proclamation, Indian Act,
Toronto Purchase, Election Day
kind of slut!

Justin untrue dough,
dough, dough, dough
it's all about the fucking
dough for you.

And I like it!
You know how it turned me
on, when you spread
Terra Nullius wide open, and
broke her with your
pipelines.
Ohhhh . . .
the tar sands, the crude oil
You know how to get me wet.

So please
Talk dirty to me.
Say my name.
Say it loud and clear.
GEN-OHHHHH-CIDE!
Yes, yes! OH! OH!
OH, CANADA!

Recording: JUSTIN TRUDEAU-IMPERSONATOR. *Through his "speech,"* MS. REDACTED *becomes increasingly aroused.*

VOICE-OVER: Uh, um.
Respect.
UHHH . . .
Indigenous!
UMMMMM.
Canada!
UHHH . . .
RECONCILIATION!

Lights out on MS. REDACTED.

Lights up on TUHI, *who mimes rolling a joint through her speech.*

TUHI: Anyway.

SCENE SIXTEEN

TESTIMONY: FRAUD AND COMPLACENCY CONTINUED

TUHI: I am trying to tell my friend about this, and she says to me, "Oh, you know.
I've never really thought about it.
It just doesn't seem that important."
And I had no idea what to say to her.
Perhaps I should have told her.

SCENE SEVENTEEN

DOUBLE-HEADED SERPENT PART TWO

LEE (projection) continues her story of the Double-Headed Serpent: the protagonist (a young boy) travels to meet the serpent with the intent to destroy it and so save his people. Ultimately, he and the Double-Headed Serpent make a treaty: the people will honour the Serpent by displaying representations of the Serpent on their house fronts and by feasting for the Serpent each year. For its part, the Serpent will protect the people.

Video ends. Lights up on CANDY.

SCENE EIGHTEEN

TESTIMONY: YOU ARE BEAUTIFUL

CANDY: I used to be afraid of white people
But it was a white woman who saved my life.
I had just turned eighteen when I made the decision to kill myself.

That year, I lost my uncle. He was my teacher. He taught me a lot about fishing, and when he passed, he left me his whole fishing box and the fishing spoons he had made for me.

In that year, I lost my friend. He was so young, but he was a healer to me. He never judged anyone.

Then, I lost my auntie. She was my muse. She taught me painting and left her supplies for me.

And my dog passed away that year. Max. He held my heart, my secrets, and my pain.

Finally, my grandmother passed. She was my stone—my connection to culture. I remember that whenever I had a tummy ache, she would brew me her special tea. Then, she'd lift me up to the bells hanging in her kitchen and tell me to ring them. Every time, the ache went away immediately.

Anyway, I had moved down to Tío'tia:ke ("Montreal") for school.
My financial situation was bad,
Academic pressures were intense,
I hated living in the loud, polluted, negative, fast-paced city,
My landlord was fuckin' inappropriate.
The racism had become an unbearable norm.

"Guess what, Mr. Willmer? I passed the York University auditions!"

“Oh, how will you pay? Oh, that’s right, you’re gonna go talk to your tipi.”

So, one bitter December afternoon, I made the decision and crafted a perfect, painless plan. Classes had finished, and I was on my way out to get morphine from a friend. Walking down the hall, I thought, for the last time. And I hear, “You’re so beautiful!” from an older white woman walking towards me in the hall.
“What’s your name again?”
I told her my name, and she told me hers
I had never met this woman in my life!
She invited me to tea, and I went.

I can swear my Ancestors were watching over me. My grandma!

Tummy ache.
Heartache.
Morphine or Tea.
Morphine or Tea.
Morphine or Tea.

I came so close.

Kind words.
Good intentions.
Strong Tea.

Powerful medicine.
Love medicine.
Life-saving medicine.

So, when I tell you that you are beautiful today, know this . . .

My grandmother spoke through that white woman I met by chance on the last day of my life, and my days were lengthened.

I see your beauty through their eyes, and so, perhaps, your own days will be lengthened as I send out their medicine to you.

> CANDY *moves to stand behind* TUHI.

You are so beautiful today.

> *Lights up on* TUHI *and* CANDY *above and behind them.* INDIGENOUS CAST *enters: they take their places on stage in "irreconcilable space." They are in shadow.*

SCENE NINETEEN

TESTIMONY: FRAUD AND COMPLACENCY CONTINUED

TUHI: Perhaps I should have told her.

PESCH: Everything happens for a reason.

CANDY GIRL: What happens to me happens to you.

SARAH: What happens to you happens to me.

JENNIFER: We all have a responsibility to this land.
To educate
To dismantle
To centre Indigenous Peoples
To be accountable.
Know your history.
Know thyself.

TUHI: Hydrogen bonds keep us glued together, a silvery thread of empathy, growing stronger as our understanding of each other weakens.

CANDY: Need peace. Miss peace.

TRINA: For 150 Years.

CANDY: Need peace. Miss peace.

NON-INDIGENOUS CAST enters. Members take their places in "irreconcilable space." A loose semicircle is formed by Indigenous and non-Indigenous members of the cast. The sharp borders between the two groups are somewhat blurred in this configuration. CANDY moves to sit on the stairs stage left. PESCH sits on the upstage riser centre.

SCENE TWENTY

TESTIMONY: FAMILY WIITIGO STORY

TRINA: When I was a little girl, I was *always* hungry, always hungry. And I was *always* holding a baby. Me and my little brothers and sisters, there were so many of us. We were always hungry. We had to help our mother because she was always being abandoned by our father. He'd survived residential school, and the Second World War, and he wasn't well. He was always leaving us to fend for ourselves.

My mother was a good provider. So strong. Such a wonderful hunter. But one harsh winter, we ran out of meat. And we were all so hungry! Our mother could see us suffering. So, she said to us, "Come on, kids, let's go, come on let's go! We're gonna load up, and we're gonna go to the winter camp. Maybe we'll find something in the traplines there. Come on, load up!" So, we got excited, and we got filled with hope, and we thought, "Oh, maybe we'll eat tonight! Maybe some good meat!"

So, we loaded everything up, all of our bedding, and our good canvas tent, and my mother's rifles, and the knives and our cookware, all the things that we would need. And I got the baby, and I loaded my little brothers up. And my mother, she climbed in. And off we went! I loved watching my mother—the way she drove those horses! "Yaaah! Yaaah! Yaaah!" It was fantastic!

When we got to the winter camp, our little cabin, we unloaded everything—our bedding, our cookware, our stove. We were so tired and so hungry. So hungry.

So, my mother checked the traplines while I took care of the baby and told stories to my little brothers. (We're gonna eat tonight!) But when my mother returned, we could see the disappointment on her face. There was nothing in the woods. And she saw how hungry we were, so, she said, "Come on, kids, let's load up again. We're gonna go just a little bit further. Just a little further north. I know there's good hunting out there." So we did. I said, "Come on, little brothers, let's load up again." So we took all our bedding and we put it in the wagon, we took our stove and our rifles and the knifes. And we thought, "We're gonna eat. We're gonna eat, for sure!" And my mother climbed into the wagon and off we went. "Yaah! Yaah! Yaah!" We were so excited, we're gonna eat tonight. We came to a clearing and my mother said, "This is a good place, let's pitch the tent here." So, we did, we pitched the tent up and we put the stove in, and we put our bedding down, and I got my little brothers to lay down to go to sleep and my mother said, "Okay let's sleep. We're all so tired. In the morning, I'll hunt. I'll hunt something for us." I was so happy to give that baby over to my mother so that she could nurse the baby all night. I was so hungry and tired.

So I laid down in my bed, and just as I was ready to fall asleep, I had to pee. But it was cold, and it was dark outside, and I was scared. But I didn't want to wake anyone up to come with me. I said to myself, "I'm a big girl, I can do this! I can go pee by myself!" So, I put on my mukluks, and I put on my coat, and I peeked out of the tent—

Gesture: opening tent flaps.

—and I looked out into the dark.

I saw the horses, and I thought, "Maybe I'll go pee next to them." Except they were acting very strange, they were moved their ears back and forth like this, listening intently. And their eyes were bulging, and they were blowing, "shhh shhh," blowing into the ground. And they were looking around, and their skin was shivering. They were bumping into each other, trying to comfort each other. And I realized that they were afraid. Something had frightened them. And I started to feel their fear.

And I wondered why they would be afraid: there can't be any bears around. The bears are sleeping! Oh no! Maybe it's one of those big cats in the trees! So, I looked around at the trees, and as I looked, I started to get that feeling, that something was watching me. My skin was crawling, I felt something watching me. And, as I looked in the trees, on a tree branch, it was the Wiitigo! And he was looking down at me. His flesh was hanging from his bones where he'd eaten himself. And his mouth! He was still gnawing on his lips. And he was gnashing his teeth, and he looked at me and did this *(Wiitigo teeth)*. And I could smell him! He smelt horrible! Rotting flesh! I was so scared! I just wanted to get on one of the horses and get away from that place!

But I knew I couldn't leave my mother and my little brothers behind. So, I very quietly and very carefully went back into the tent, and I woke my mother. Nikawi, Wiitigo! And my mother sat up. She could see the fear in my face. And she said, "Shhh, we have to leave this place. Wake your brothers quietly." So, I did. I woke my brothers and I said, "Shhh, we have to get out of this place. Quickly. Quietly. Let's go. Get your things." So, we quietly put everything back into the wagon, we took the tent down, and my mother said, "Keep your heads down. Don't look up!" We put the tent back in the wagon, and the stove.

And my little brothers were so brave: they went out and they got the horses, and those horses were so scared they pretty much backed themselves right up to the hitch. They wanted to go! They wanted to get out of there. And my mother.

"Yaah! Yaah! Yaah!" We flew through the night! We flew through that snow. And you could see the wheels behind us kicking that snow up as we left that place. And as we got further away from that place, we could feel that evil leaving us. We were leaving it behind.

TRINA *continues as slow fade begins.*

We were so happy when we got back to the cabin—so relieved. But I felt terrible. I wondered, "Why did I see the Wiitigo? Why did the Wiitigo come to me?" I asked my mother, and she gathered us around her and told us she had to apologize. She said, "This is not your fault, my girl. My children, I'm sorry. This is my fault. I took us too far. I took us into sacred land. Land that is to remain untouched. Land that is to be kept for our future generations."

We hear TRINA's final words in the blackout.

"The Wiitigo came to us, to remind us not to be greedy. And to only take as much as we need. There's enough good hunting here. I just wasn't being patient."

SCENE TWENTY-ONE

GRATITUDE WEAVE: RECLAIMING INDIGENOUS VOICE

Projection: Borden Building North, University of Toronto.

JENNIFER: When I saw my name on an office door at the U of T
I thought to myself, yup, I've made it.
Jennifer Alicia Murrin
A young, queer, mixed kid from K'Taqmkuk with her name on an office door at the prestigious U of T.
Wow!
First on my dad's side of the family to even attend university, and now I'm working at one?!
My family thinks I'm so smart.
I am thankful to have an office with green walls and a window facing Ishpadinaa.
Grateful to have a job
Privileged to work with brilliant Indigenous folks every day.
Immersed in Indigenous knowledges, worldviews, traditions.
Witness Indigenous and non-Indigenous students learn Anishinaabemowin.
Kanien'kéha
Thanksgiving Address.

PESCH gestures.

PESCH: Everything happens for a reason.
Once, I sat on an edge like this.
Once before.

CANDY sings her version of the Thanksgiving Address in Kanien'kéha. As PESCH testifies, CANDY's Thanksgiving Address becomes a direct response to her call.

It was a bridge that overlooked a deep ravine. I could see a small creek at the bottom, so far away.

CANDY sings her Thanksgiving Address.

I wondered how easy it would be to let myself go, to fall.

CANDY sings Thanksgiving Address.

But I couldn't. I thought about my family, and my friends, and my sister.

INDIGENOUS CAST: Sister. Sister. Sister. *(echoes)*

PESCH: I thought about my boyfriend Terry. He died when I was eighteen, jumped off a bridge just like that. He was revived by the paramedics, put on life support but was pronounced brain-dead. His sister called me that night, and I was so shocked. She asked me to come to the hospital, they were taking him off life support the next day. I woke up early and left to catch a bus. The bus driver was looking at me.
"Why do you look so upset, what's wrong?"
"My boyfriend is in the hospital. I'm on my way to say goodbye to him."

"Was it an overdose? That happens a lot to you Natives, right? Like all the alcohol and drugs in your communities and violence."

"SHUT THE FUCK UP! You don't know anything! Who do you think you are?"

Everything happens for a reason.

PESCH gestures.

So, a couple months after Terry's funeral, his sister Candice, who had become my best friend, said we should get tattoos. She got one with Terry's name, his birth date and death. She suggested I get something similar. But I didn't feel like I was important enough to have his name on my body. So, I was wracking my brain, stressing as I tried to think of something, when it hit me. A memory of a text message. One of the last things Terry said to me.

"Ha ha! I love you! I'm so glad I worked at that hellhole for six months 'cause then, I got to meet *you*. See? Everything happens for a reason."

PESCH gestures.

And I knew that's what I wanted.

For five years after that, I struggled to deal with his death. Depression, suicidal thoughts, and alcohol were running my life. I was spiraling downward. I felt hopeless and stuck. Who could help me? I knew I needed to get out, but I didn't know how. Then one day, my friend Cheyenne messaged me. Said she was moving to Toronto for theatre school. "Take me with you!"

BRENDA: Take me with you!

JENNIFER: Take me with you!

PESCH: And she did.

We came to Toronto together. I couldn't believe I was actually here, seeing all the buildings and the CN Tower. I spent the next four years at the Centre for Indigenous Theatre. I had so many classes.
Like Improv
Clown
Movement
Singing
Stage combat
Acting for Camera
I found my voice in Solo Playwriting.

BRENDA softly begins to drum and sing her Cree Woman's Song.

JENNIFER: Legends
Traditional ecological knowledges
Smudge whenever we need medicine
Celebrate with songs
And laughter
And feasts
It is truly a beautiful thing.

BRENDA continues singing her Cree Woman's Song.

CANDY GIRL: Everything happens for a reason.

PESCH: I found my voice. I found my voice!
All of the news I was hearing about Indigenous youth committing suicide in Attawapiskat and mascwacis.

INDIGENOUS CAST: Aamjiwnaang
Big Trout Lake
Kehewin
Cold Lake
Saddle Lake
Georgina Island
Muskrat Falls
Thunderchild
Starblanket
Batchewana
Wikwemikong
M'Cheeging
Duck Lake
the Pas
Shawanaga
Pond Inlet
Kanawake
Kanasatake

Oneida
Six Nations
Odanak
Garden River
Kitigan Ziibi
Poundmaker
Toronto
Vancouver
Montreal
Edmonton
Christian Island
Iqualuit
Winnipeg
Scugog
Curve Lake
Rice Lake
Rama.

PESCH: EVERYWHERE! And so, I knew I wanted to write something to help inspire change, so these youth know that death is not the way, that there is hope and there is a brighter future.

The Cree Woman's Song continues. MELANIE, TRINA, *and* CANDY GIRL *have joined their voices with* BRENDA*'s.*

JENNIFER: Legends
Traditional ecological knowledges
Smudge whenever we need medicine
Celebrate with songs
And laughter
And feasts
It is truly a beautiful thing.

CANDY: Everything happens for a reason.

CANDY *gestures.*

PESCH: That's why I came to Toronto.

The Cree Woman's Song stops.

JENNIFER: Yet our songs cannot drown out the remnants of what was here before.
And sometimes, when I sit at my desk, I swear I can hear the walls talk
And wonder what they need to say.

KATIA: I'm so, so, so sorry.
I swear I didn't mean to.
So don't put this on me.
I'm telling you.

Between you and me, I'm contaminated.
I carry a disease.
The G-disease, it rhymes with tide.

CAST: Genocide, genocide. *(whispered echoes)*

KATIA: Tidal waves of bodies.

CAST: Genocide, genocide. *(whispered echoes)*

KATIA: By nature, I am a protector, a nurturer
I want to . . .
But by nurture, I've been made a murderer too.

CAST: Split mind *(echoes)*

KATIA: Witness of our sins
Piled together
A reminder

JENNIFER: I swear I can hear the walls talk
And wonder what they need to say
What we need to hear

Maybe it's the voices of children
Who were exposed to nutritional experiments
Reminding us every time we feast to make them a spirit plate
Maybe it's the voices of children who went to residential school
And were taught by teachers who were trained here
Or maybe
It's Garrison Creek bubbling up from the tunnels
Anxiously wanting to break free
To be unrestricted
Natural.
Every time I look out my office window at Ishpadinaa
I am also reminded of this.

And some days those truths are heavy.

ANDREW: My professor defended her dissertation in the house that Sir John A. Macdonald occupied in the year that the Indian Act was signed into Canadian law. I see her struggle to keep from weeping as she tells us how, years before, her own professor told her that she was a "barbarian savage who belonged in a factory and not a university." That for years, she has been "missing," and that she is now in recovery from soul-death.

CANDY: Then, she smiles. Wipes her tears. And in Odemin Giizis, we share strawberries on the lawn of that house, and we fill our mouths with sweet medicine from the earth and remember what it is to be brave.

TRINA: My professor sometimes passes a brick around the room for each of us to hold as she tells the story of the Train of Tears that Sir John A. MacDonald built and the school that swallowed generations of her family whole.

PESCH: Then, she smiles. Wipes her tears. And shows us what it means to be a teacher, an artist, a poet, a scholar.

TUHI: My professor has received death threats.

CANDY GIRL: Still, her office door is always open.

JENNIFER: My professor has no access to clean drinking water in her home.

SHARAI: Still, her children are clean, healthy, and happy.

CANDY: Still, she fights like a mamma bear to keep her students safe and flourishing while we learn.

TUHI: My friend survived the Sixties Scoop.

GRACE: My friend survived the Millennium Scoop.

KATIA: My friend is *not* missing.

TRINA: My friend is an architect

MANNAN: A doctor

CANDY GIRL: A language warrior

SHEILAH: A writer

CANDY: A dancer

URI: A water protector

JENNIFER: And some days I wonder why we know the milk-white history of the Borden building, but not the full story.
And what business I have working in this institution.
What responsibilities come with knowing these truths.

ANDREW: How do strangers become friends? How do we embrace contradictions of life, of friendship—the contradiction that results in growth, renewal, resurgence?

PESCH: Once I sat on an edge like this before.

MANNAN: At the edge of the woods

URI: At the water's edge

SARAH: This is not the first time this has happened.

BRENDA: For 150 YEARS.

CAST: For 150 years *(whispered echoes)*

Lights change. SARAH *stands alone front and centre—on the edge.*

SCENE TWENTY-TWO

RE-ENCOUNTERS AT THE 'EDGE OF THE WOODS'

APOLOGY ACKNOWLEDGEMENT

SARAH: Standing here at the edge of the edge of the woods
I tiptoe softly
Humbled by your power
Your compassion, your radical love rage
The beauty in the actions you have shown me
Born trespasser and complicit in your pain.
And I want to answer your beautiful call
And respond to your rightful demands for change
Because I pray your great-great grandchildren into existence
And until everyone knows this is Indigenous land
I want to be part of the resistance.

From the weight of the burdens you have been forced to carry
Because people who look like me
Have the privilege of not caring
Not standing up
Not speaking out
Not looking at our own role
In this genocide
And I want to be part of the solution.
This apology comes deep from my insides:
I'm sorry that you didn't want to cry in front of settlers like me.

Though we have done you and your family harm
And caused sorrow through generations
I find it so disarming
That you're concerned for my comfort
And catching me if I fall
While I'm intruding in your space
The ghosts of your ancestors in the walls

May they all be set free
From the shackles
Of the Train of Tears
And the ever-present fears
Of violence
That make Indigenous youth take their own lives.

While we just turn a blind eye
To the rape of your land and people and water
That we're still committing—
Physical, spiritual, and emotional—
While blaming you
And calling you names like "Barbarian Savage"
When in truth you're the most brilliant artist, who is magic!

Powerful survivor
Incredible force of nature
And role model
For whom I hope to be some day
Reaching out a hand to me
And even letting me be in your play.

I'm sorry to all of you from my past self
Too busy drowning in her own trauma
To reach out a hand to you
While knowing that you needed help
To stop this oppression in its tracks.

But what constitutes a good apology?
If I don't show you actions,
Why should you swallow the potential
For yet another promise broken?
How can I be accountable to these words
I have just spoken?
I'm still learning—a flawed human
But I will keep showing up in uncomfortable moments
moving through them.

I'm not asking for forgiveness
And it is not your job to give this
But I'm holding out a hand
Asking humbly for a chance
To sit beside you and listen
With the same letters as *silent*
Like we tried to make you for so long
Forcing you to speak English
And banning your dances and songs.

But your sound could never be buried
The original caretakers of this land,
Far too powerful you are
And I'm sorry for everything we have done to you
And the still throbbing fresh wounds, and scars.

Energy and sound never die
So, I can't erase the sordid past
And present
To make them go away.
But I can start
By standing aside
While you reclaim a stolen sound.

> *BRENDA softly begins to sing her Cree Woman's Song. Gradually, the INDIGENOUS CAST joins in.*

> *Projection: MELANIE's Land Acknowledgment plays as live MELANIE sings BRENDA's Cree Woman's Song.*

MELANIE: *(projection)* Miigwetch for the calming scent of the waawaaskoneyin. It grounds me. Miigwetch for being strong enough to hold our house, soft enough for tiny toes, wise enough to teach us, loving enough to fill out lungs, and forgiving enough to welcome my family into partnership with you.

Video out, slow fade.

NON-INDIGENOUS CAST: Miigwetch. Miigwetch. Miigwetch.

Blackout.

Cree Woman's Song: Iskwewuk

BRENDA I. WASTASECOOT

Iskwewuk **waniskak**! (Women, wake up)
Iskwewuk waniskak Iskwewuk!
Wayahay, Wayaho! Wayahay, Wayahay, Wayaho!
Iskwewuk, **niipawik**! (Women, stand up)
Iskwewuk niipawik . . . Iskwewuk!
Wayahay, Wayaho! Wayahay, Wayahay, Wayaho!
Iskwewuk **bimoothdek**! (Women, walk)
Iskwewuk, bimoothdek Iskwewuk
Wayahay, Wayaho! Wayahay, Wayahay, Wayaho!
Iskwewuk, **nigamook**! (Women, sing)
Iskwewuk, nigamook Iskwewuk
Wayahay, Wayaho! Wayahay, Wayahay, Wayaho!
Wayahay! Wayahay! Wayaho!
Wayahay! Wayahay! Wayaho!

This Cree Woman's Song "Iskwewuk" calls upon women to take back their mind and body, to reclaim their whole self, so that they can stand up to violence around them and sing with power and pride! I sing this song for all Indigenous women who fight for a better life for themselves and their children.

This Cree Woman's Song came to me after some months of working on a similar song with my colleagues at Brandon University in the First Nations & Aboriginal Counselling Degree Program. I sang this version of it at a Native women's retreat at the Jessie Saulteaux Resource Centre in Beausejour, Manitoba. There, I met women who had been brutalized most of their lives by their partners, brothers, fathers, strangers, and pedophiles. One woman's story got to me, and my heart really went out to her. I can't repeat her story, but I just want to say that when we are the listeners for our sisters, we can be moved to act in powerful ways. My voice, though shaky, sang this song with the drum I had made with my daughter from our teacher, Mae Louise Campbell.

This song also comes from my lived experience, my mother's, and my aunt' experiences. The words are sung in Cree. Iskwewuk means women; it speaks to all women, not just Cree women. The song urges them to waniskak! which means to wake up from their sleep. The sleep refers to our sense of hopelessness, when we just stay in the abusive relationship. Niipawik means stand up to violence in our lives, and bimoothdek means to walk out of that place of powerlessness. The last verse has the word nigamook, meaning to sing. We have voices, so let's use our voices and sing together. This is how we will heal ourselves and our communities.

Myself, I lived with that kind of abuse, and it took me almost a decade before I could leave for good. There came a critical point of violence at the hands of my husband. And I had to make a choice. Then, I had a daughter to think about; it was not just me anymore. I had to stand up and walk out of there. It was a very frightening time for me, but I had to think more about my daughter, who was then two years old. The decision to leave came from a flashback I had as I was laying on the floor, being strangled. The flashback was from when I was around two years old and finding my mother on the floor and my father on top of her punching her repeatedly. Her words still haunt me to this day, "Nipahiin! Kyam, nipahiin!" That means, "Kill me! Go ahead! Kill me!" These were the words of defeat or the pleas of the precious women in my life.

In that flash I decided I wanted to live and be here for my daughter, therefore I would not be saying these words. Instead I asked him, "Where's our daughter?" and that's what woke him from his blind rage and he relaxed his hands from my neck and let me go. Today I am a grandmother and I sing this song with other women and in my classrooms to encourage other women to find their power, to find their voices.

Experience of Witnessing

BEKA MORRISON

Today is 1 July 2022. It has been 155 years since Confederation. But as we all know, the land that we now know as Canada has been inhabited since time immemorial by the Indigenous Peoples of this land. My name is Beka Morrison; I am a settler—of Irish, Scottish, and Ukrainian descent—living in Guelph, Ontario. Guelph is situated on the ancestral homelands of the Anishinaabe, specifically the traditional territory of the Mississaugas of the Credit First Nation, in Treaty 3 territory. I graduated from the University of Toronto in 2020 ,where I studied drama, theatre, and performance before going on to complete a graduate certificate in arts management at Humber College. Since I first saw *Encounters at the 'Edge of the Woods'* three years ago during my undergrad, there has been a movement in this country and a larger conversation surrounding reconciliation because of the tragic discovery of 250 unmarked graves at a residential school in Kamloops, British Columbia. At the time of writing this, the number of unmarked graves that have been located has risen to 2,301, and the media has stopped covering the story. As a settler, I don't know or fully understand the feelings of pain, grief, and intergenerational trauma that this discovery has brought forward or intensified. However, witnessing these events and the fallout has reminded me of my experience of witnessing *Encounters at the 'Edge of the Woods'*– of seeing the impacts of colonialism and having to come face to face with my role and responsibility in shouldering reconciliation as a settler. My family may have only been in Canada for a few generations, but they were able to come here and establish their lives thanks to the displacement and genocide of Indigenous Peoples. That's how I have the life I have now, and seeing the fallout of the graves and watching this show are two things that have forced me to spend time reconciling this fact.

Having spent a semester in Jill Carter's class discussing Indigenous storytelling and reframing the way we see theatre and performance through a *de*-colonial mindset, set me on a path of considering my place as a settler in a colonial state and as an artist. How do I view life and art through a decolonial lens? How do we break from the mould of Western forms of storytelling? What is the story of the land I live on? These were the questions I left Jill's class with and took with me to my viewing of *Encounters at the 'Edge of the Woods.'* To say this show was a theatre experience I had never had before would be an understatement. Even now, almost three years later, I can't quite find the words to express my experience watching this show aside from the fact that it shaped how I see art in a new way. So long I've been stuck in a way of experiencing art through tropes and climactic storytelling. But to see a show that was created as a team rather than within a hierarchy and by experiencing how each actor's story and performance stood on its own and connected into the larger story of the show, really showed the point of story-weaving. It shows us as individuals who actually gives and creates within the larger story, causes us to see ourselves as a part of something larger; from my experience, Indigenous Peoples are much better at seeing themselves as a part of a larger collective picture and story than are settlers—especially white people. I have never seen that so clearly before than when I watched this show. Since graduating from school and moving into the professional theatre world, I've reflected on what I learned in this show and in Jill's class, and how Canadian theatre needs to shift and change to be a space that reflects this country now and all that comes with the reckoning of the last few years. As the Canadian theatre scene changes and grows, I hope to see it make increasing space for stories like *Encounters*—storytelling that centres the voices of Indigenous experiences and traditions that don't always follow a colonial narrative structure but take stories that we need to hear and weave them into each other so we can see for ourselves how everything connects to each other.

I learned more about Canadian history in this performance than I did in any of my history classes. I think that speaks to how far we all have to go before we can consider a real effort being made towards reconciliation. I have been taught so much about colonizers coming to Canada and have been fed the Kool-Aid about happy friendships and the fur trade while spending only a week in Grade 10 History studying residential schools. Never were we told about the Sixties Scoop. Never were we taught about the stewards of the land upon which we were learning; never were we taught to think about how Canada, as we know it today, is so young—that our history isn't so far in the past. It is living and breathing and impacting us all right now. Here. Today. These aren't the things you can just learn from a textbook and hope to remember by the time your next test comes around. I spent time in Jill's class learning about the land in which the University of Toronto was built upon. A part of the story of that land to which I felt very connected was the history of the lost waterways of Toronto. Under the university runs three waterways that were lost to the construction—one even being polluted and buried by former students of the institution in what is now called Philosopher's Walk. It's a certain irony that a place named for people within society that we often think of as the smartest among us hides something that was lost due to the lack of care for the land we live and learn on; the loss of one of our most precious resources is not something I would connect with being smart.

As white people and as settlers, we need to expose ourselves to this. We have to seek out art and stories like *Encounters at the 'Edge of the Woods,'* and listen to what they are saying. Multiple times in this show it is stated that "you can google this shit," and that's true. We are all victims of a lack of knowledge perpetrated on us by the Canadian government. So, if you hear about something like the mass graves on the news or someone's Instagram story, take it upon yourself to google it. Educate yourself. Take the emotional labour off Indigenous Peoples and find reliable sources to learn how to better support Land Back initiatives and Indigenous Peoples. If you make the choice to attend post-secondary education and take part in academia, question what you're learning and where the sources are coming from. So often these institutions are run by old white men. Most of my history minor was taught by old white men. These are not the people who can speak faithfully to the experience of colonialism because they are the ones who benefit the most. The systems of education and academia are set up to distort our image of nationalism and history. Experiencing Indigenous art and including Indigenous history in the classroom and academic world challenges power structures and allows a wealth of knowledge to be erased. The information is out there; we just need to give space to those who hold the history to pass it on so we don't repeat the mistakes of our ancestors.

I am grateful to have had the opportunity to witness this show, especially in a space that for 100 years had been the stage for colonial art on Indigenous land. This show impacted me in ways that I will be forever grateful for. I'm excited for others to experience it, love it, and see the ways that they can self-reflect and work towards change. This show was the result of the work of an incredible group of people who put their hearts and souls into every story told, and it creates a show that everyone deserves the experience of witnessing.

The Uncomfortable Moment

SARAH MICHAELS

is it better to say the words you need
as perceived by me
and plant a seed
of accountability
if i'm scared
if i mess up
i know it feels weird
but if silence is violence
and i say the wrong thing
am i helping you fly
or clipping your wings
should i ask what you need
instead of assume
but it's not your job
to see my words through
it's mine to keep digging
and doing my best
you've laboured so long
i know you need rest
is it work then,
to even listen to me
when i say i have an apology?
have i centred myself
when it's about you?
you deserve your land back
we can't do what we do
continued oppression
and violence and crime
then post orange shirt pics and say
"oh, it's fine—
i posted about it so i'm a good folk"
hiding behind the veneer of being

social media "woke"
i don't know what's best
and it's not about me
perfectionism can't prevent this
apology
it must be set free
from us white ones who've fucked up
it can't be your chore
is attempting to make 'amends'
hurting you more?
is intention to heal
impacting more breaking?
the souls of your ancestors
must be rage-shaking
at what we have done
to you through generations
is a sliver of "sorry"
enough communication?
without actions to back up
i know it's just words
don't know all the right ones
just through what i've heard
so what's best moving forward?
some might still be confused
but we can't let that make us
just let you feel and be used
control is still something
we whites must surrender
can't take it wrong
if you don't praise the sender
after decades of delays
and our many faux pas
i'm still sorry for everything
with all my flaws.

When I originally had the privilege of participating in *Encounters at the 'Edge of the Woods,'* I had no idea what I was getting into. All I knew was that Jill, a person whom I love, admire, and respect, asked me if I would like to participate, and it was an unequivocal yes. I didn't know what, if anything, I had to contribute. I just knew it was an honour to be asked and an honour to be there.

Over the process of our shared creation, it became clear that my presence as a settler was having an impact on some of my Indigenous castmates' feelings of safety in the space. I was always afraid to say the wrong thing and often did. I felt really stupid as one of the only people in the non-Indigenous cast who wasn't studying Indigenous history in university. I had my own trauma that I was working with as well as COMPLEX POST-TRAUMATIC STRESS, but I also realized that many of my Indigenous castmates had experienced similar trauma on top of genocide and racial oppression over generations. Needless to say, the rehearsal period felt very intense.

The inspiration for the poem came from a pure moment of raw emotion—someone saying they hadn't wanted to cry in front of me because they didn't want to make me uncomfortable. I was a visitor in *their* sacred space. They were unpacking and processing severe injustices and emotionally charged traumatic events and just my presence made them feel like they needed to repress their own feelings for my comfort level.

This absolutely broke my heart because, after such a brave outpouring, the person had a right to a safe place, and I was making them feel unsafe.

I could leave, but that wouldn't solve anything. They could leave, but that wouldn't solve anything. I couldn't automatically make them feel safe, but I could acknowledge what was happening and apologize for it, even though I didn't know how to "fix" it. So that is what started the written words of what eventually became an apology piece in *Encounters*.

Each line of the piece was based on a personal experience or story from another cast member, a real person as opposed to just some vague idea of "those people over there." I think it really highlighted the fact that this work is deeply personal. Indigenous Peoples are not just an idea from a history lesson. They are living, breathing, amazing, powerful people who deserve to be witnessed and to experience our shared humanity. They bestowed this humanity on me with such kindness and grace that it left me in awe. Any edits to my slip-ups in terms of words or ideas were suggested gently and patiently.

It seemed clear that a genuine effort and action made clumsily with mistakes was better than a choice to ignore, to not care, to run away.

One of the lines in the poem is a promise that I will "continue to show up in uncomfortable moments, moving through them."

This is one of those uncomfortable moments. I don't know what I'm doing. I'm flawed. I'm white and aware of my privilege but sure I'm still messing up. I don't want to be silent when it's important to speak up, but I don't want to be performative with some kind of empty social justice post and no action to back it up. I want to educate myself but don't always know how to.

But if I have learned anything about showing up, it's that it is ultimately about our shared bravery. The bravery to admit the truth of how you're feeling, the bravery to listen, the bravery to genuinely try to connect even through discomfort or an energetic clash, the bravery to respect boundaries, and the bravery to try again.

Showing up can take many forms. It's never going to be perfect, and it is never going to be over. There is no quota of actions to take to get to a finite end point. Healing isn't linear, and showing up is not a one-time act. It doesn't have to be a massive thing done by one person or institution at some future date—in fact, this will never work—it is all of our responsibility, and it can start right now with those closest to you. Sometimes it feels amazing, and other times it feels like shit. The thing about that is, shit makes great fertilizer. By continuing to show up even when it feels uncomfortable, we can create a rich soil from which trust can slowly grow, one interaction at a time.

Chi Miigwetch for allowing me to show up to the page today and for sharing your sacred space with me once again.

About the Contributors

Susan Aaron collected and recorded some of the sounds required for the pre-show installation for *Encounters*. She is an environment-based researcher looking at engagement with nature's biodiversity in relation to sustainable creativity most often in a city. She is an EdD candidate at the Ontario Institute for Studies in Education at the University of Toronto.

Abdul Mannan Ahmad graduated with a BA (Hon.) from the University of Toronto in 2021. Based in Toronto, Mannan is an actor, writer, and director.

Nicole Eun-Ju Bell is a mixed-race, multidisciplinary artist with a passion for performance and technology. Among other things, she is a projection designer, stage manager, and Extended Reality artist. Her work has been presented at international festivals, such as the Prague Quadrennial and many festivals and venues in Toronto.

John Kim Bell is Canada's first Indigenous symphony orchestra conductor, the founder of the country's precedent-setting National Aboriginal Achievement Foundation and the National Aboriginal Achievement Awards (today known as Indspire and the Indspire Awards), and one of Canada's leading energy resource consultants representing Indigenous Nations in Canada. An internationally recognized leader and activist in the arts, philanthropy, and Indigenous resource development, Bell is an Officer of the Order of Canada and a member of the Order of Ontario. Other honours include the Royal Bank Award for Canadian Achievement (1988), three medals from HRH Queen Elizabeth II, and other citations for his ground-breaking work. In 2003, he was named the National Outstanding Cultural Leader (Canadian Conference of the Arts); in 2005, he served as one of five Canadian advisors to then Prince of Wales, Charles; and he received a Lifetime Achievement Award from the Royal Conservatory of Music in 2007. In recognition of his contribution to the advancement of Indigenous Peoples, John Kim Bell has been honoured with three Eagle Feathers throughout his career. Mr. Bell is also the recipient of the 2023 Ramon John Hnatyshyn Award for Voluntarism in the Performing Arts. The Collective Encounter is very grateful for his support and most honoured that he agreed to write the foreword to this book.

After serving as director of the English section of the National Theatre School of Canada from 2001 to 2012, **Dr. Sherry Bie** went on to earn her MA at York University's Department of Theatre and Performance Studies. In December 2021, Sherry successfully defended her doctoral dissertation from the Centre for Drama, Theatre and Performance Studies at the University of Toronto.

Jenny Blackbird is nehiyaw from Kehewin Cree Nation, Treaty 6 territory, and Finnish Canadian. She is Resource Centre and Programs Coordinator at First Nations House Indigenous Student Services at the University of Toronto and holds an MEd from York University. She is a hand drummer/singer, a retired old-style Jingle Dress dancer, and a multidisciplinary artist with a background in fashion design. Jenny is also producer and co-host of the *Indigenous Waves* radio show, which airs Mondays from 7 to 8 p.m. EDT on CIUT 89.5 FM. Jenny is the recipient of a 2016 Minaake Award from the Native Women's Resource Centre of Toronto, and a 2019 International Day for the Elimination of Racial Discrimination Award and 2021 Excellence Through Innovation Award from the University of Toronto.

New parent and entrepreneur, **Otsíkh:èta (Candy) Blair** is an interdisciplinary visual/performing artivist from Tio'tiá:ke (Montreal region). They had their first gallery showing at age fourteen and was the youngest artist to participate in La Nuit Blanche *Two Mountains* as Candy Ice. Candy's projects include their Indigenous Catering, which was featured in an episode of *Télévision française de l'Ontario*; creating and acting in *Money Can't Be Eaten* at the Aki Studio Native Earth; jewelry business, "O.Tsi.Sweet"; video *Accountability*, which is available at https://www.ddlsquared.rocks/20210605-accountability-music-video; various international digital pieces with queer-feminist director Antje Budde and the Digital Dramaturgy Squared Lab; the *Talking Treaties* spectacle; and Cheri Maracle's *The Story of Six Nations*. Candy aspires to continue sharing their platform and working on artistic projects involving human rights and equality. Connect with Otsíkh:èta on Instagram @3otsikheta3, or on their Facebook artist page at https://m.facebook.com/Ots%C3%ADkhÃ¨ta-1707547459492693/. Please email o.g.kheta@gmail.com for business inquiries.

Katia Café-Febrissy is a Toronto-based award-winning writer and director. She originates from Paris, France, and is of French Caribbean heritage. She's lived and worked in five different countries; in addition to English and French, she speaks Spanish and Creole fluently. Katia is a member of the Directors Guild of Canada, the Francophone Writers Guild of Canada (SARTEC), and Women in Film & Television—Toronto. In addition, she sits on the board of directors of the Liaison of Independent Filmmakers of Toronto. She is an alumna of the 2018 Women in the Director's Chair Story & Leadership program and Career Advancement Module and the Ateliers Varan Documentary Film Centre in France where she earned her postgraduate diploma in documentary filmmaking. She holds an MA in literature and languages from the Université de Paris VIII, France.

Dr. Jill Carter (Anishinaabe-Ashkenazi) works in Tkarón:to with many Indigenous artists to support the development of new works and to disseminate artistic objectives, process, and outcomes through community-driven research projects. Her scholarly research, creative projects, and activism are built upon ongoing relationships with Elders, scholars, youth, artists, and activists positioning her as witness to, participant in, and disseminator of oral histories that speak to the application of Indigenous aesthetic principles and Traditional Knowledge Systems to contemporary performance. She is a member of the Talking Treaties Collective (with Ange Loft, Victoria Freeman, and Martha Stiegman) and co-author of the recently published *A Treaty Guide for Torontonians* (Jumblies Theatre & Arts and the Toronto Biennial of Art).

Cayla Clarkson holds a BA degree from McGill University in drama and dramatics theatre arts. Her professional life bridges the worlds of arts and public health, and her professional endeavors include stage and production management, project management, and event planning.

Megan Laurel Davies is a Caucasian cis-female settler, born and raised in S'ólh Téméxw, Stó:lō territory. She currently resides in "Scarborough," located within the 1923 Williams Treaty that includes seven First Nations as signatories. Megan is an active community volunteer and works in the non-profit sector.

Currently pursuing a certificate in design for arts and entertainment from Toronto Metropolitan University, **Max Cameron Fearon** holds a BA (Hon.) from the Centre for Drama, Theatre and Performance Studies at the University of Toronto. Max is a queer-genderqueer, Mad, and disabled director, performer, and facilitator with extensive experience in community-engaged works.

Andrew Kesik is an actor, musician, and organizer residing in Tkarón:to/Toronto. He is finishing his undergraduate degree at the University of Toronto, majoring in theatre and political science. Andrew is also active in labour and student unions. When he is not on stage, you can find him organizing for free education.

Currently pursuing her doctor of law degree at the University of Toronto, **Isabel Klassen-Marshall** holds a first class joint honours/bachelor of arts degree in political science and history (with a minor in Indigenous studies) from McGill University.

Lauren Lacey worked as the assistant lighting designer and transcriber for *Encounters*. They studied drama at the University of Toronto, where they focused on playwrighting and theatre production. Their play *Cordelia* was shortlisted for the 2018 Robert Beardsley Award. They are currently pursuing their master of information in library science degree.

A member of Shawanaga First Nation, located on the eastern shore of Georgian Bay in Robinson Huron Treaty territory, **Melanie Laking** has been a part of the urban Indigenous community in Toronto for most of her life. She holds a BA in Indigenous studies from the University of Toronto. Currently, Melanie is an MSW candidate at the University of Toronto, specializing in health and mental health; a tour guide for First Story, Toronto; and an Indigenous health advocate. Melanie is a wife, mom, sister, auntie, and friend.

Uri Livne-Bar is a playwright, actor, musician, and sound designer. Having completed his theatre specialty at the University of Toronto, Uri is currently working on audio plays for young audiences with First Ditch Collective. As a sound designer, Uri enjoys recording soundscapes from the streets and neighbourhoods around his home.

Stó:lō/Cree-Métis scholar-artist **Lee Maracle** (1950–2021) was a world-renowned author, a prominent theatre-worker, an impactful mentor and educator, and a committed activist. Her publications include *Bobbi Lee: Indian Rebel* (1975), *I Am Woman* (1988), *Daughters are Forever* (2002), *First Wives Club: Coast Salish Style* (2010), *Celia's Song* (2014), *My Conversations with Canadians* (2017), and *Hope Matters* (2019), co-written with her daughters Columpa Bobb and Tania Carter. In 2018, Lee was named an Officer of the Order of Canada; in 2020, she was named finalist for the Neustadt International Prize for *Celia's Song*; and in 2021, she delivered the Margaret Laurence Lecture on "A Writing Life." Lee

Maracle's teachings, mentoring, and oratory are crucial foundations upon which *Encounters at the 'Edge of the Woods'* was built.

After working in the corporate sector for almost sixteen years, **Sharai G. Masanganise** quit to pursue full time studies at the University of Toronto, Canada. She would like to be involved in communities that are comprised of those who are disadvantaged, Indigenous, and from the African continent. Her desire is to create an atmosphere of understanding and empowerment. She was born in Zimbabwe, has lived in England, and now lives in Canada.

Sarah Michaels is a multidisciplinary artist, yoga teacher, and Reiki healer and is honoured to be a part of this project. Her published works include her original monodrama *Make A Wish 11:11* (Sorplusi Publishing under the direction of d'bi.young anitafrika at the Watah Theatre). She has also appeared in the *10 x10 Photography Project* (volume 8) as a model, photographed by the acclaimed LGBTQIA2S+ photographer/fashion designer Mikey Sin. In her free time, Sarah can be found writing poetry and cuddling cats.

Beka Morrison is an arts administrator currently based in Guelph, Ontario. She graduated from the University of Toronto's Centre for Drama, Theatre and Performance Studies with BA (Hon.) in 2020, and from Humber College with a graduate certificate in Arts Administration and Cultural Management in 2022. She currently works as a producing assistant at the Stratford Festival.

Trina Moyan is nehiyaw iskwew (Plains Cree) from the Frog Lake First Nation in Northern Alberta, Treaty 6—Medicine Chest territory. She is a multidisciplinary artist whose favourite role was playing the cannibal professor in *Encounters at the Edge of the Woods*, the first ever Indigenous play mounted at Hart House Theatre in 2020. Trina has spent her career working in front of and behind the camera, producing for both CBC and APTN. When she isn't acting she supports the Indigenous community as a member of First Story Toronto, sharing the Indigenous history of the city; a muralist with the Red Urban Nation Artist Collective; an educator and advisor at the University of Toronto's Daniels Faculty of Architecture;

and is co-founder of Bell & Bernard Ltd., a First Nations consulting firm representing the interests of Indigenous communities. Trina's life and work are inspired by her two boys and her mother, Jeanne, a residential school survivor.

Jennifer Alicia Murrin (she/they) is a queer, mixed Mi'kmaw and settler (German/Irish/Scottish) multidisciplinary artist originally from Elmastukwek, Ktaqmkuk (Bay of Islands, Newfoundland), now residing in Toronto. Find out more about her work at jenniferalicia.com and on Instagram @eastcoastjam.

Tash Naveau is of Denesuline/Chipewyan (Deer Clan) and Eastern European descent and a member of the Anishnaabe community of Mattagami First Nation in Treaty 9 territory. She is an auntie, screen-based arts worker, and side hustle artist. You learn more about Tash's work by visiting @tashnavo on Instagram.

Pesch Nepoose is a Cree multidisciplinary artist from Edmonton, Alberta. Now based in Toronto, Pesch is a 2019 alumna of the Centre for Indigenous Theatre and works professionally as a multidisciplinary performer, stage manager, and tour guide. Recent projects include *Mno Bimaadziwin* for Theatre by the Bay; her one-woman show *The Bridge* for the Paprika Festival and Weesageechak Begins to Dance; and the films *Dish Dances, By These Presents* (Talking Treaties Collective), and *Hunger* (which premiered at the Imaginative Film Festival 2019). Pesch enjoys working with Clay and Paper Theatre, Jumblies Theatre, the Collective Encounter, Out of Sync Collective, and many others.

Born and raised in Tkarón:to, **Grace Phan-Nguyen** is a film producer and theatre-maker based in Berlin. Their current portfolio focuses on a wide range of digital creators of colour. The experience and teachings from this project have continued to inform their work and have led them to pursue documentaries and food-history projects that focus on human connection. Back in Tkarón:to, they were previously the arts management intern at Nightwood Theatre, one of the coordinators of the Ad Hoc Assembly, and administrator for the Arts Consultants Canada/Consultants canadiens en arts.

Born in Manila, Philippines, **Sheilah Madonna Mortel Salvador** has lived on Turtle Island for decades now. Her work as a writer and facilitator has been greatly affected and inspired by her Indigenous studies and social justice programs at the University of Toronto. She is committed to helping other underprivileged and marginalized BIPOCs through knowledge sharing, storytelling, and creative artistic expression. Connect and stay in touch with her on Instagram @sheilah_madonna_.

As a first-generation immigrant to Canada at the age of four, **Tuhi Sen** is deeply moved by the potent history and immediate reality belonging to the Original Peoples of this sacred land. Participating in the creation of this work brought many important gifts into her life—friendship, learning, and awareness are but a few. She is interested in the power of community and the sharing of personal stories to help guide collective healing and clearing the pathway to holding each other in greater compassion. *Encounters* was her introduction to the practices of story-weaving and devised theatre. In her writing and acting work (which are on their way, just stuck in a wee bit of cosmic traffic), you will always be able to find the little sliver of *Encounters* that lives within her heart. Please connect with her on Instagram @tuhisen.

Gabriele Simmons earned her BA (Hon.) with a specialist major in women and gender studies from the University of Toronto in 2017. In 2021, she graduated from the Ontario Institute for Studies in Education with an MA in adult education and community development. Gabriele is a highly proficient grant writer for the Toronto and York Region Métis Council, a passionate social-justice advocate, and a poet, dancer, and choreographer.

Shirka Urechko is a Canadian settler and multidisciplinary artist of Ukrainian English heritage. She is a student of the Indigenous studies program at the University of Toronto and is a member of the sound design team for *Encounters at the 'Edge of the Woods.'* She has been involved in the arts for many years, first as a performer and choreographer of dance theatre and now as a sound designer and writer. She is as a member of International Alliance of Theatrical Stage Employees Local 873's Scenic Department in Toronto and has worked on television productions such as *The Boys*, *Reacher*, and *Chucky* for Amazon Prime Video as well as Guillermo del Toro's *Cabinet of Curiosities* for Netflix.

Dr. Brenda Wastasecoot is a member of the York Factory Cree Nation, raised in a Cree-speaking family in the Flats village at Churchill, Manitoba. Brenda currently teaches at the Centre for Indigenous Studies, University of Toronto. Her interest in community theatre began in her search for healing childhood sexual abuse trauma. She joined Adults Molested as Children in Brandon in the early '90s and found acting to be the most effective way of releasing long-held grief and shame. She's always loved the arts, and music and theatre has been a long-held passion. Working in collaboration with the Collective Encounter has been a blessing in her life. Her publications include *Showing and Telling the Story of Nikis: An Arts Based Autoethnographic Journey of a Cree Adult Educator* (ProQuest) and *Granny's Giant Bannock* (Pemmican Publications).

Dr. Hallie Wells is a multidisciplinary writer, editor, and writing coach. She holds a Ph.D. in sociocultural and linguistic anthropology from UC Berkeley; her academic work bridges anthropology and poetics. She was a magazine editor in her pre-Ph.D. life, and in her current editing and coaching practice she loves supporting scholars in making their ideas shine. She is a staunch advocate for karaoke, bike lanes, and the serial comma.